GRAND STREET

Cover: Robert Rauschenberg, *A Doodle (Borealis)* (detail), 1990

Grand Street is set in New Caledonia by TeX Source, Houston, Tex., and printed by W. E. Barnett & Associates, Houston, Tex. Color separations and halftones are by Color Separations, Inc., Houston, Tex.

Grand Street (ISSN 0734-5496; ISBN 0-393-30742-5) is published quarterly by Grand Street Press (a project of the New York Foundation for the Arts, Inc., a not-for-profit corporation), 135 Central Park West, New York, N.Y. 10023. Contributions and gifts to Grand Street Press, a project of the New York Foundation for the Arts, Inc., are tax-deductible to the extent allowed by law.

Unsolicited material should be addressed to the editors at *Grand Street*, 135 Central Park West, New York, N.Y. 10023. Manuscripts will not be returned unless accompanied by a stamped, self-addressed envelope.

Second-class postage at New York, N.Y., and additional mailing offices. Postmaster: Please send address changes to *Grand Street*, Subscription Service, Dept. GRS, P.O. Box 3000, Denville, N.J. 07834.

Subscription orders and address changes should be addressed to *Grand Street*, Subscription Service, Dept. GRS, P.O. Box 3000, Denville, N.J. 07834. Subscriptions are $24 a year (four issues). Foreign subscriptions (including Canada) are $34 a year, and must be payable in U.S. funds. Single-copy price is $8.50. *Grand Street* is distributed to the trade by W. W. Norton & Company, 500 Fifth Avenue, New York, N.Y. 10110, and to newsstands only by B. DeBoer, Inc., 113 E. Centre St., Nutley, N.J. 07110.

GRAND STREET

Editor & Publisher
Jean Stein

Managing Editor
Barbara Heizer

Art Editor
Walter Hopps

Assistant Editors
Elizabeth Osborne
Erik Rieselbach

Designer
Don Quaintance

Researcher
Paige Crowley

Copy Editor
Kate Norment

Advertising Director
Chris Calhoun

Contributing Editors
Morgan Entrekin, Jonathan Galassi, Suzanne Gardinier,
Andrew Kopkind, Maria Margaronis, Edward W. Said,
Robert Scheer, Jean Strouse, Katrina vanden Heuvel,
Shelley Wanger, Drenka Willen

CONTENTS

Amy Tan
Peanut's Fortune *10*

Jimmy Santiago Baca
Love Poem *23*

Ben Sonnenberg
Upstaged *30*

Rosanna Warren
Le Ventre de Paris: A Marriage Poem *38*

Julio Cortázar
A Rejected Chapter from *Hopscotch* *40*

Aaron Shurin
An Exhibition *55*

Robert Rauschenberg
Seven Works on Paper *(portfolio)* *57*

Herbert Woodward Martin
The Washerwoman's Fire *73*

Kazuo Ishiguro / Kenzaburo Oe
Wave Patterns: A Dialogue *75*

Kenzaburo Oe
The Way of Eating Fried Sausage *92*

Charles Wright
Maple on the Hill *113*

Peter Nagy
Time Lines *(portfolio)* 115

Sarah Gorham
The Minor Manchu's Daughter 129

André Gorz
What Way Is Left? 130

Eric Ormsby
Mutanabbi in Exile 165

Linda Connor
Egypt *(portfolio)* 167

John Hollander
Days of Autumn 178

Richard Powers
We Are Climbing Jacob's Ladder 182

Grover Amen
On the Runway 204

Fernando Pessoa
Fragments from *Livro do desassossego* 206

Michael McClure
Disturbed by Freedom 216

About the Cover 218

Contributors 219

Illustrations 224

Peanut's Fortune

The marketplace was already crowded at eleven o'clock that morning, and everyone was doing a good business. And all this busyness raised my excitement even more. That day even the woman who sold soup from the front of her house did not have to cry out, "Wonton! Try some, best wonton!" Both tables were full of people with cold red cheeks poised over steaming bowls, and a dozen more were squatting on the ground, bowls balanced between their legs.

We passed the usual stalls that sold fruit and vegetables, eggs and live chickens. But that day, the fruit looked bigger, the chickens more lively. Red banners hung everywhere. Firecrackers exploded at every step, and babies were screaming as their mothers reached for pears and oranges, pomelos and persimmons. Little Gong and Little Gao were watching a monkey dancing. At the end of the show, they threw two coppers on the ground. The monkey picked them up, bit them to see if they were true, tipped his hat to the boys, then handed the money to his owner, who gave him two dried lizards that he crunched right away. We all clapped.

And then Peanut found a fortune-teller she liked, a fat woman with a big smile who promised she knew everything— love, marriage, wealth. A sign in front of her stall bragged that she had the luckiest fortune sticks, knew all the lucky numbers,

the right lucky marriage combinations, the best days for making lucky business decisions, remedies for changing bad luck into fantastic luck. Everything guaranteed.

"Little sisters, ah," she said to us, then patted her stomach. "See how rich and fat I've become following my own advice. I don't need to do this to make my living, not at all. I do this only because the Goddess of Mercy asks me to, to advance myself in the next world. So you see, my good fortune for you does us both a favor. Come see, best fortune, hanh, I can prove it to you."

And then the fortune-teller did a remarkable thing. She said to Peanut, "Your lucky number is eight, isn't this true?"

And Peanut remembered that she was born in the eighth month, that her eighth year had been especially happy, and that she would be eighteen as soon as the new year came. And so, with half her mouth dropped open and half the money New Aunt had given her, Peanut bought a fortune that promised that within the year she would marry a man who would make both her parents happy. Her mother-in-law would be too good to be true. Her future household would have enough riches that she would never desire anything else. And, of course, she would have many children, one right after another.

"What will my husband look like? Not too old, I hope," Peanut said in her complaining voice. "And where does his family live? Will I have to stay here forever at the Mouth of the River?"

The woman picked up another stick, then frowned, looked puzzled. Another stick, more frowns, and then another. "Mm," she said. "Your husband is young enough, it seems, only a few years older than you. But your destined family lives close by here, that's what I see. This is not too bad, but perhaps I can make it better for you."

After more money was exchanged, the woman wrote Peanut's name on a piece of red paper, along with her birth date and the date of the fortune, then added a piece of paper with some sort of rhyming poem. It went something like this: "Happiness comes from nearby, as far-reaching as the East Sea."

"What does this mean?" Peanut asked, after reading the rhyme.

"Ah," said the woman, and held the poem close to her eyes.

Finally she pointed to the words "nearby" and "happiness," and said, "See this? This is the local man you were supposed to marry, but now I've chased him away, sent him to someone else." And then she pointed to the words "East Sea." "And this means your new husband is someone who lives farther away— not as far as another country, of course, but not from this island. Maybe as far north as Yangchow."

Peanut had an ugly scowl on her face.

"Maybe as close as Shanghai," the woman said. And when she saw Peanut smile, she added, "That's what I see. And riches beyond imagination. Five sons, all of them dutiful. And no other wives, you are the only one."

The woman put all the slips of paper and the poem on top of a golden tray, along with Peanut's money, and laid this in front of a statue of the Goddess of Mercy.

"Now there are no more worries in your life," the woman told Peanut. And then the fortune-teller smiled at me. "But how about you, little sister? I feel there's a husband in your future too."

And then she peered at my face, looked at me closely, and her mouth dropped open. "Ai-ya! But look, there is a problem, I can see this now, sitting right above your eye! This little speck here, it can make everything you see turn black."

And she pointed to the mole just above my eye, below my eyebrow. "I can fix this," she said quickly. "It is not easy, of course, to find a charm to fix bad fate. But I can do this for you, remedy this before the new year. Your decision." She wrote down a number, the amount I should pay her.

But Peanut was already pulling my elbow in another direction, telling me she had heard about a stall that sold foreign-made chocolates shaped like all twelve animals of the horoscope. Of course I wanted to hear my fortune, get my charm, change my bad-luck future. But how could I say this in a crowd—"Eh, Peanut, give me money so I can find a better husband too"?

Maybe that fortune-teller could not have told me anything to change my fate. Maybe she used only the most ordinary tricks and nothing she said was genuine. But what she said was certainly true about me: unhappiness was coming my way, and I did nothing to keep that speck from blowing into my eye. And

this came true as well: Peanut did not marry the local boy she was supposed to get with the first fortune. She married someone from Shanghai. And the local boy she chased away with a rhyming poem? Those leftovers went straight to me.

No, I'm not being superstitious. I am only saying that's how it happened. And how can you, my daughter, say luck and chance are the same thing? Chance is the first step you take, luck is what comes afterward. Your kind of chance makes no sense, it is only an excuse not to blame yourself. If you don't take a chance, someone else will give you his luck. And if you get bad luck, then you need to take another chance to turn things from bad to good. Of course everything is connected.

How do I know? Well, you can see for yourself—one thing was said, then the same thing happened. We lost Little Gong and Little Gao, then we found Wen Fu. I did nothing about it; then . . . well, here's what happened.

We were looking for Little Gong and Little Gao, walking through the marketplace. Peanut scolded them as if they were there: "Bad boys, always getting in trouble. Why don't you listen to your big sister?" We walked from one stall to another, pushed our way through the thick crowds, always looking for them, unable to rest our eyes for even one moment on interesting trinkets.

At last we found them. They were standing at the front of an audience, everyone waiting for a play to begin. The audience was enclosed in what looked like an arena partitioned off by ropes. A big sign over the stage said, "A New Year's play in honor of the god of the village. Debtors welcome."

"You remember this," I said to Peanut. "Same as last year." And we decided to stay with the boys and watch. This was the mock play the village people put on on the last day of every year. The same old tradition. In the old days, if someone owed you money, you could chase him down and make him pay. But only until the last hour of the last day before the new year. After that, too bad. So landlords and merchants were always running after poor people, chasing them until dark. And the only safe place a poor person could go was to this play, a play dedicated

to the god of the village. As long as you stood inside the roped-off area, nobody could demand payment from you.

Of course, it was still true that you were supposed to pay your debts before the end of the year. That was the honorable thing to do. But now the village play was only for fun. And the people inside the ropes were not really debtors; they had been pushed inside to become part of the play itself.

I can still see and hear it. Cymbals and drums sounded loudly, and actors in cheap-looking costumes appeared on the stage. An old woman walked on, sweeping a straw broom, crying over her lost son, the bandit. Off in the distance a dragon was rising out of the sea, his tail rippling like waves. The dragon was bellowing about his hunger for the ships of greedy men. These were two operas all mixed together, awful.

Suddenly the actors stopped what they were doing. A beggar man in a tattered jacket jumped up from the audience and went running up and onto the stage. He raced around the old woman and the dragon, grabbing a broom, grabbing a tail, crying to someone behind him, "I don't have your money! I swear it!"

Another man jumped out of the audience, this one holding a lantern high in one hand. "Ah!" whispered the crowd. "The evil landlord!" He too rushed across the stage, and three times almost caught the beggar—by his hair, his ear, the tail of his tattered jacket—but the beggar managed to spin away each time. The audience roared with relief and laughter.

The actress playing the old woman pretended to be annoyed. "Stop! Quiet! We are performing an important play," she cried, and as the two men whirled around her again, she threw her broom at them, but missed—ponk!—striking the dragon's tail instead. More laughter! And then the man holding up the tail of the dragon peered out, rubbed his aching head, and asked, "Where am I?" The audience laughed even louder.

Then more shouts: "Make way! Stand clear!" And two men in the audience were pushing everybody back. One moment later, the beggar ran off the stage, sprang onto his hands, then bounced forward three times, head over heels, before landing within the safety of the ropes. The crowd clapped. The landlord with the lantern was now on the other side of the ropes, stomping his feet, while everyone jeered at him.

Little Gong and Little Gao did not tire of this until the whole scene had been repeated two more times with different acrobats playing the beggar and the same actor playing the landlord. At the very end, the landlord was so mad he broke his lantern in two, then announced he was going home. "Forget the debt," he shouted. Everyone cheered in victory, as if they too had won. But as the landlord started to walk away, he suddenly turned around and called to the audience, "I'm going home, it's true, but all of you now owe our fine actors a token of your New Year's generosity!"

And then all the actors jumped into the audience with begging bowls in hand. The tail of the dragon was nudging Peanut, and he turned out to be Wen Fu. He must have thought Peanut would give him a big donation, to judge by the way he eyed her fine clothes and called her "generous lady."

Let me tell you, he was not the kind of man that would make you say, "Oh, this man is very handsome. I should marry him." Not like your father. But Wen Fu had a way that made your eyes follow him right from the start, a manner that was unusually confident, very bold. When he said "generous lady," his tone sounded so sincere, yet his face was teasing: turtle eyes that blinked slowly but did not look away, a wide grinning mouth. He was—how do you say it here?—charming.

And there were other things I saw about him, which Peanut later told me she noticed too—signs that he was raised in a good family, that he was elegant, a person you did not have to look down on. His clothes fit him well, everything falling to the exact length of his arms and legs. And he wore Western-style clothes: a wide-collared shirt, open at the neck, and tailored pants with a thin belt at the waist and sharp cuffs at the bottom. His hair was full and shiny, cut neatly all around, not stringy or chopped off at the bottom like a farmer's. His eyebrows—we both liked his eyebrows. They were thick and nicely tapered, like two ends of an ink brush. And he had strong-looking teeth, all straight, not one tooth missing in front.

He held out a small money bowl. "Not for me," he explained again in that soothing, sincere voice. "For the hospital we are building at the south end of the island." His eyebrows rose up in the middle, a look of concern. He looked at Peanut, then

at me. Of course, I was embarrassed that I had no money to give. So I gave him a stern look instead, as if he should not be bothering us.

Peanut smiled at him. "Such hard work to be a dragon," she said. And then she gave him a few coins, and we both turned to walk away. But now Wen Fu was calling to Little Gong and Little Gao: "Hey, little brothers, I have some lucky money for you in return." He pulled out two red money envelopes from his pockets and tossed a packet to each of them. In a moment, they discovered the envelopes contained some sort of candy in the shape of coins wrapped in gold foil. "Are they real?" Little Gao cried and held one up to the sun, watching it shine. They put their coins back in the envelope with much respect.

"Thank you, Uncle," they said.

"Did you see how well I worked the dragon tail?" Wen Fu asked them. They nodded shyly, smiled. "Maybe you would like to see the whole dragon?" And then they threw all shyness away, jumped up and down, and ran to the stage. Wen Fu looked at Peanut, then at me, and shrugged as if he had no other choice.

For the rest of the afternoon, Wen Fu followed us. Or rather, he led the boys to see different sights—a cockfight, a game where wooden boats were sunk by sand bombs, a stall that claimed to sell tiger teeth—and we were the ones who followed. Of course, we protested at first, saying, "No more, you've already gone to too much trouble." But I think both of us secretly thought he was exciting. We sighed as if we had no other choice, then giggled because we did not know how to express our excitement any other way.

He carried our packages, spent his own money on little treats for the boys. And then he tried to buy things for Peanut and me, luxuries he saw us admire—a paper dragon on a string, a chocolate candy, in the shape of a sheep, that Peanut had been eyeing. "You should not do this!" we protested each time. Or maybe only I protested. Peanut just smiled.

So you see, I never took those gifts from Wen Fu. Peanut did. She said she would tell her mother she bought them herself, so many good bargains. But I knew this was wrong, not just the lying but taking something from a man. There were many sayings about that: "Take even one sweet, and lose your whole life to

bitterness.'' ''Eat forbidden candy and your stomach pops out.''

And I could see how those sayings were right. Something was already happening. Wen Fu was winking at Peanut, his ink-brush eyebrows dancing. All afternoon it went like that.

You have an American expression for what Wen Fu did to Peanut: ''He swept her off her feet.'' That's what he did, exactly that. At the end of the day, when Peanut complained that her feet ached like two burning coals, he found a farmer willing to rent his wheelbarrow for a few coins. And then he lined the dusty insides of the wheelbarrow with his own jacket, and invited my giggling cousin to ride home in her new sedan. As he pushed her home, he sang to her, happy songs, sad songs, songs about secret gardens and dark pavilions.

By this time, most of Peanut's white powdery face had rubbed off onto her coat. And I could see her cheeks were as flushed as mine. She was happy. And I can admit this. I was sick in my heart, such a bad feeling.

You see how he was? Always flamboyant, showing off in a big way, just like the actor he was that day. Charming!

A man with good manners would have found a pedicab. He would have secretly paid the driver before we knew it, then sent us home. Or maybe he could have shown his concern by inviting the girl and her cousin to rest a little, to take some simple refreshment at a teahouse. He would not have remarked about her feet, how small and delicate they looked, no wonder they were tired. And a good man would not have played favorites, filling one girl's heart with pride, the other's with envy. And whatever interest he showed, he would never have asked the girl for anything in return.

But Wen Fu asked. He pushed Peanut down the road. He saw our big house. He saw the banners for our celebration. He asked to come in four days, the third day of the first month of the lunar new year, to pay his respects to Peanut, her family, and, of course, to me.

The next day was the new year. Everyone pretended to be happy and kind, shouting, ''Ten thousand generations!'' ''Long life!'' ''Highest position!'' ''Biggest prosperity!'' That sort of thing, all meaningless, but good-sounding.

The servants were especially happy, because they did not have to work that day. All the cooking was done, and now no knives could be touched, no sharp words could be thrown. We ate sweet things and cold dishes.

Peanut and I talked about Wen Fu, wondering if he would come in three days. We wondered what kind of house he lived in on the other side of the island. We wondered if his mother was too good to be true. I did not say anything to Peanut about the rhyme she had used to chase this local marriage away.

The next day Peanut woke up crying. She said she must refuse to see Wen Fu! How could she see him? He had seen her when she was a vision of beauty, with her face powder and lipstick on, wearing her most sophisticated clothes. She could not put powder on her face, wear that in front of her mother and father. She could not show Wen Fu what she looked like underneath. I tried to tell Peanut that Wen Fu would find her even more attractive when she looked natural. I did not say this only to be kind. It was true. If he liked her when she looked ridiculous, why should he not like her the other way?

But I could not convince Peanut in time. When Wen Fu came, she hid herself. She was there, of course, watching him from different hiding spots: the top of the stairs, behind the door of a dark room, through the windows of the greenhouse.

And then Old Aunt and New Aunt met Wen Fu. He called to them in such a sincere voice, "Auntie, Auntie," as if this were a happy reunion. At first they were puzzled. They could not recall who he was. Then he presented them with a basket of expensive fruit. He sent respects from his mother and father, especially his mother, who seemed to be a longtime friend of Old Aunt's. Eventually Old Aunt thought so too. She struggled with her memories until she found one that matched. "Ah, you are Mrs. Wen's son. Only a little baby the last time I saw you, I think."

I heard this and laughed. I admired Wen Fu. If I had any good feelings for him in my entire life, it was at that moment, maybe a few others like that. He was so bold, so clever, funny, and daring. So you see, even now, I can still remember a few good things about him.

Lucky for Wen Fu, the house was soon filled with hundreds

of people, all the villagers who had come to eat *nian gao*, the sticky rice cakes with a name that sounds like you are saying "happy new year." So if Old Aunt and New Aunt were confused by Wen Fu's visit, it seemed only a natural part of the day. Too many people to keep track of anything.

I was ladling out bowls of boiled dumplings when Wen Fu approached me. "Where is she?"

"She's shy," I said.

"She does not like me?" he asked. His eyebrows were pushed into a frown, but he was smiling.

"Only shy," I said again. It did not seem proper to confess that Peanut liked him.

"Why suddenly shy?" he said with a laugh. "Does shy mean she likes me?" And then he turned to me. "You aren't shy? Does this mean you don't like me? Ha! Is this the case?" He had that same teasing look.

I almost could not answer him. "I'm not that way—that is, not shy."

"So perhaps you also like me," he said right away.

"Being shy does not mean you like or not like," I said.

On and on we talked that way, until my head hurt from trying to be polite, trying to hide from his tricky questions. Finally he pulled an envelope from his pocket.

"Little sister, please give this to her," he said. "Please tell her to answer me tomorrow." And then he left.

Peanut had been watching all along. So when Wen Fu left, she dashed out from behind the kitchen door and demanded the letter from me.

"What does he say?" I asked her. I felt I had as much claim on reading the letter as she. I had worked so hard for her. Peanut hunched her shoulders over the letter, protecting it from me the same way a mother duck places her wing over her babies. She was giggling, biting her fingers, squeezing her fist, pulling a strand of her hair.

"What does he say?" I asked again.

Peanut looked at me. "He needs an answer tomorrow," she said. "Tell him I have no answer yet. Tell him to wait." And then she walked away.

So I helped Peanut and Wen Fu: carried their love letters

back and forth, to the marketplace, to the middle of our road. I was helping them to each other. I did not have it in my mind to steal Wen Fu away from Peanut. I swear this. I am not remembering this differently to avoid blaming myself.

Each time I delivered a letter to Wen Fu, I used my words to carry a picture of Peanut to him. I told him what color dress she was wearing that day: rose-colored, the same as her cheeks. I reported how she had put a little decoration in her hair: a dragon pin, thinking about him. I hinted that she was unable to eat and was becoming thin.

Of course, none of this was true. I was only using my imagination to talk about all those silly, lovesick things girls did for romance back then.

So how did I come to marry him? Sometimes I think about asking Peanut. If she is still alive in China today, she would agree, I'm sure of it. I did nothing to make Wen Fu turn his eyes and look at me, nothing at all. Wen Fu changed his own mind.

I had a good heart, just like you. I was innocent, just like you. So maybe you can understand how your mother once was: a lonely girl, a girl with no expectations, wanting so much. And suddenly someone came knocking at my door—and he was charming, a reason to dream about a better life.

What else could I do? I let him in.

Love Poem

We threw the wounded fragments
into the middle between us—
 what we feared most to tell each other
 we told.
 Emptying our mouths of all the dark nights,
 emptying our bodies of all the pain,
 emptying our hands of all weapons,
 we piled the fragments between us
 the way soldiers surrender their rifles
 to the resistance.

I remember the first year I made love the way you liked it:
 a sun-shower
 on the seed
 opening to flower.
But over the years my love changed
 from rain to
 hail. I saw it yesterday:

 two horses in the field
 leaned to escape the stinging pelts,
 tried to get in front of each other
 to shield themselves from the burning,
 and then the hail brought them to their knees.

 I come blue and soft, then pass
 through cold regions and turn to hail,
 and you cringe, seek escape, lie down.

I remember gripping my mother's thighs,
suckling at her breasts,
entangled in her hair,
clutching at her,
 and now my body seeks that connection with you.

Now at the window, where I saw the horses go down,
 I watch you drive away
angrily, seething gravel from your tires,
 and the cord snaps.
I see your blue car turn at the stop sign
 and you're gone.

In the horses' strength and dignity,
 in those front legs bending,
 in the quivering flanks
 trying to deflect the burning beads,
 in the dark crevice of the knees,
 finally giving up all hope,
 I saw us.
The hail shredded the flower.

• • •

But the first year—
I didn't mind
building the fence till my hands bled,
cropping the vegetables in the garden till my knees bled,
stuccoing the house in March winds till my lips cracked and bled.
I gave thanks
 for our lives together.

All this winter I have been coughing.
Love makes me old and discontent gnaws

and gouges my lungs.
I used to love you, woman—
 the way a wolf's tongue thrusts up to catch bluebodied raindrops,
 my tongue darted between your legs.
Full mornings we lay in bed and I softly bit your flesh
 the way a jaguar cub gnaws the spindles of his cage.

When a coyote howls his maleneed call for his mate,
with tensile gait loping buoyantly at the crest of dunes, profiled against the moon,
I see her come,
 and I want to howl for you,
 but instead I curse:
 "What the fuck you want me to do, bitch!
 I don't need this shit from you!"

I remember the first year—
when I touched you, a thousand bees filled my fingertips!
Your nipples were pomegranate seeds
and all summer my lips were red!
Your laughter oceanwaved,
shaking free the nets inside me!
Oh, our bodies moved to each other,
wind-pushed flames burning through brittle prairie grass!

But what has happened to us?
I clench my knuckles
 and I want to leave.
My eyes shimmer with anger.
We have not held each other in a long time.
This has been a homeless winter for me.
 I want to leave
 my land, my children, my beliefs, my gods,

and you . . .
and become someone else
in another place and time.

Clouds part and moonlight
spreads on my side of the bed. I stare
at the moon. I can't reach over
and touch you,
can't kiss you,
can't hold you,
can't make love with you,
because my touch draws pain from you
the way a rose-picker's hand
brings in only barbs
from green stems.

Hail shreds the flower
and brings the horses to their knees.

●　●　●

And after days of hate,
 what do we do?
Make love on the floor.
My body sings in the pre-dawn color of your skin
like old bells on Andean peaks at dawn,
in so much silence and solitude,
 beating
 I am alive I am alive I am alive.
The male dance of the bell sounds in my male dance.

●　●　●

Grandma taught me how to suck poison from a snake bite:
"Chew the skin good, chew good, then suck and spit, *mejito* . . .

increase the hurt, widen the pain,
 touch the darkness,
 see and feel the poison.
 It is the dark work of life.
Go down into the wound,
work your healing,
then spit the poison out.''

This love is a fish hook
 in my thumb.
 I can't pull out the barb,
so I scrape around the hook
with a pocketknife,
 widen the hole, increase the pain,
 all of myself uttered in pain of the moment—
as I cut the hole rounder
blood pours, what I am made of
hurts, I dig deeper,
 work my healing
 then pull the hook out.
I extract it, clean and easy,
and have learned.

 • • •

Man rage is the unpicked fruit rotting on the branch
man rage is wanting to turn the steering wheel into the oncoming tractor trailer
man rage is the boy's terrified face when his parents divorce
man rage is the shame of not being able to pay bills and working at a job
 against your values
man rage is when yelling is normal
man rage is when you want to spit in your wife's face
man rage is having no words to express fear

man rage is when you don't give a fuck anymore about your body
man rage is hunger in the guts to know why you feel this way
man rage is the brass door knocker and no hands to knock
man rage is the house with empty rooms
man rage is the fear the wife will take everything
man rage is the clock on the wall looked at every day by a spouse serving a
 hundred years
man rage is the housing market with divorcee homes to sell below market cost
man rage is the son suing the father
man rage is the man beating his wife because his parents beat him
man rage is the basketball player dying on the court from cocaine
man rage is when you stop answering people and stare into your hands
man rage is days filled with wordless departures and slammed doors
man rage is the disease that leaves a man no dignity or decency
man rage is breakdown and death if we cannot express it.

• • •

We men are returning home,
 rising
 from our dying
 to live over again
 with our children.
Men are returning to their children.

I fix my sons' swing set, tighten screws on the slide,
I change diapers, sitting on the toilet,
 while my other son stands in the doorway
 next in line for my lap.
I move and they follow,
I cook and they eat,
I sleep and they wake,
I sing a new man to them.

They stand in my male shade, I purr my jaguar growl,
 they crouch and grunt and leap at my chest,
 my hands are ripe fruit they nibble,
 I sniff, they paw, we skip and leap
 across the living room, wrestling, dancing, yelling,
 healing,
 we hug-wrestle,
 spin and jump and scamper and land on all fours.
 My children leap and laugh with me
 in our male song, Ahoa, Grandfather!
 Ahoa!

Upstaged

I am a Collectors' Child.

I was born in New York City, on the thirtieth of December, 1936, and was brought up in a very grand private house, 19 Gramercy Park. It was crammed with servants, furniture, and art.

Until his death in 1978, my father was one of the best-known public relations men in America. He described his business as "making giant plinths for little men to stand on." In fact, his clients were often large, powerful corporations, and his services to them were different from the flackery that his description implies, more commonplace, more corrupt. For his services he was paid, as he said, "*scandalously* well," and we all lived in a showy, extravagant, public way.

Our home was a stage for my father's work; when he was home, he was changed by whatever role he was playing. He wasn't the same as he was on our walks. Giving the provenance of some painting was different from telling the story of a city building. And the stories of uptown buildings: how impersonal. "That is where Joseph Pulitzer lived. A tunnel runs under the street from his house to that of his mistress. . . ." He narrated a city different from that of Grand and Henry streets. "That is the Brook Club. They don't let in Jews . . . The Racquet and Tennis Club: no Jews . . ." I came to know much of uptown New

York in terms of whether the buildings there were or were not "restricted."

His way of walking when he was uptown was nimble, on the balls of his feet. In and out of restaurants, galleries, shops, fleetly, sometimes impolitely, he was always a patron, a customer. Downtown, by contrast, his progress was that of a big man in a small village, slow and a little flat-footed, hands down by his sides, awaiting obeisance, tribute, petition. There he was what he was. Not that he wanted for deference uptown. Once, in fact, in the 1960s, in Central Park, we crossed paths with a young policeman who saluted my father, "Good afternoon, sir." Even then, policemen weren't so civil, as a rule.

Self-made, self-taught, and self-assured, on the whole he shared little of his self with others. I used to think he shared most with me. On our walks, and when he was angry. He got angry with me about money. I stole money from him from when I was six to when I was in my twenties. He carried only new bills. A stack of these, to the thickness almost of a building brick, lay on the marble counter of his dressing table, along with his keys and pocket watch. As a rule, I was careful never to take more than a couple of bills, none larger than a ten. Once, though, early in my life of crime, I took six five-dollar bills. I was found out. Tell your father, my mother said. You have something to tell me? my father said. *Never!* I said, Prometheus preparing his defiance of Zeus. He'd taken off his jacket and was pulling off his shirt before lying down for his afternoon nap. Tell me, he said. My mother said, Tell your father. He took off his pants and underpants. *Never!* Naked, he hit me in the face. I said nothing. He hit me again. I was knocked to the floor. His belly swayed with the force of his blow, so did his balls. Ben, said my mother.

From this time on, I began to expect only the worst from my parents. I loathed them, and so overvalued even the least show of kindness.

Impressive as my father was, my mother was impressive too—in the mode of Joan Blondell. Her favorite locution was the wisecrack. "People open up to your mother," my father said.

"Clams open up. People break down," she said.

People *did* open up to her, though. She was funny—when high, hilarious—and people trusted her. It is also true that she broke people down. The more impregnable they acted the more efficient she was at breaking them down. She called it *telling truths.* "Let's tell truths," she said to me sometimes, smelling of drink, before a big formal party: important clients, rich men and women. She enjoyed her reputation for outspokenness.

But her great gift was to meet sadness with story and calamity with anecdote. I can still hear her saying, "You know, sad as it was, I couldn't help thinking of when . . ." And I could imagine her saying to the SS man on her way to Auschwitz, "I always hate changing trains, don't you?" I know that to this habit of hers I owe my own habit of cutting away to a story or joke when faced with strong feeling.

My sister wasn't impressive, not to our parents at least. Helen's favorite locution seemed to be the yawn. "Be impressive," our father berated her. "Don't sell yourself short. [Yawn.] Look at Mary McCarthy. [Yawn.] Stop selling yourself short. Let them know you went to Vassar. [Yawn.]"

Our mother berated her: "Get more fun out of life. Be happy. [Yawn.] Let boys know you like luxury. Look at Gene Tierney. [Big yawn.]"

"Don't cry. Please don't cry," I'd say to her. (Did she think I was berating her, too?) "You're impressive to me." Never more so than when you're crying, I might also have said. Depression, menstruation, breasts: these were impressive to me. But how to console her? I used to get into trouble just so she could speak up for me and forget she was sad. Yet only our mother and father could make her truly happy. Theirs was the power of memories of a close family life ten years before I was born, and of money of course.

The first of many sad—sad, sad, oh! uncannily sad—women in my life, Helen was also the first older woman I wanted to take me into her bed. I was four and she was fourteen. I lay close against her. All of a sudden, she made me get out of bed. What had I done? Premonition of a lifelong bafflement.

I was most impressive. At seven years old my favorite form of expression was the epigram. Did you do that? they'd ask of some naughtiness. How could you? And I'd reply, "My virtue

is too exalted for the vulgarity of words." I used to stammer if asked to explain myself. Once I said, "An imposing character like mine is built on reserves, not on revelations." As I grew older, I got fat. By the time I was fifteen I weighed almost three hundred pounds. The fatter I got the more insolent I was, and the more insolent the more avid for someone weak to push around. Servants were good for that, some of them. My favorite activities were masturbating and eating and reading, sometimes in that order.

"An impressive-repulsive disorder. Impress, repel. An impressive impressive-repulsive disorder. Impress, repel. Impress, repel," said one of the parody psychiatrists I was taken to as a child.

Women's sadness filled my childhood, Helen's most of all. My mother's sadness, though chronic, was easier for me to take away. Just get her to tell a story. Her sadness came from her having been brought up an only child. That always poisonous blessing was made worse in her case by a miraculous birth. Here's a story she liked telling: "There was a time when there were no governesses. Can you imagine that? Mothers took their children with them everywhere they went. One summer Sunday afternoon, long before I was born, my mother took her daughter to Gouverneur Hospital to visit a sick friend."

"You aren't an only child?" I said.

"Just be quiet and I'll explain . . . The little girl was bored, so, to distract her, a well-meaning nurse rolled her ball down the corridor. The French door at the end of the corridor was open, the ball rolled out, the child followed it and fell in the street and was killed. My mother lost the use of her legs and was paralyzed until I was born."

In later life, no good fortune came as a surprise to her. None satisfied her, either. Not my father's wealth, or his celebrity, or his influence; not the admiration of others, or even their adoration: all was her due. She liked telling of how defiant she had been as a girl. Once, when she was sixteen, she put makeup on in the ladies' room of a downtown department store and went with a girlfriend to the Blue Grotto restaurant on Mulberry

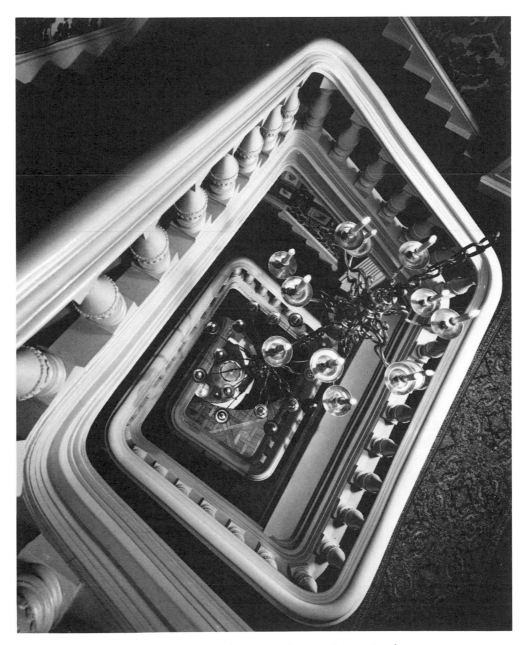

Grand stairway, 19 Gramercy Park (designed by Stanford White)

Street, where gangsters used to go. "The waiter came over and told us that the gentleman in the corner wanted to buy us a drink. I looked at him, and he didn't look like a gentleman to me, so I told the waiter no thank you, and the waiter said, 'Lady, no one says no to Louie Lepke. . . .' Now, if only your sister could be more like that."

For me, at least, my mother was never the spirited and defiant girl of her stories. Not when male authority was present. I remember this incident, after Helen went to college.

A pair of diamond earrings is missing, I'm accused of stealing them, and I'm questioned by a New York City detective and an investigator from the insurance company. We're alone in the small downstairs dining room.

"We have ways of making you talk," the detective says to me. I am ten years old, but his threat makes me feel like Brennan of the moors.

Emboldened, I say, "Then I'll tell you that a gang forced me to do it."

"Show him your fish," the insurance cop says.

"My what?" says the city detective.

"Your fish. Your tin," the insurance cop says.

The detective shows me his gold-and-blue badge. "We call this our shield," he says to the insurance cop.

"We always used to call it a fish."

"The gang is the Dukes," I say to them on my way out. "Their leader is Norman Schwarzkopf." The Dukes must have come from *The Amboy Dukes*, a favorite "dirty" book of the time. Norman Schwarzkopf was a name from the radio program *Gangbusters*, which at the end gave the names of the FBI's most wanted men. "Don't try to apprehend these dangerous criminals yourself, but call your local FBI or Colonel H. Norman Schwarzkopf of the New Jersey State Police."

Afterward my mother asks how I liked being questioned. "Very interesting," I say. "The city cop was smarter. He was strict but fair. Where were you?" It turns out that she was upstairs questioning one of the upstairs maids.

"Did she confess?" I say.

"No, but I fired her anyway," she says. And why had she let me be questioned? "Well, you said it was interesting, didn't you?"

I say, "Yes . . ."

And she says, "Well, there you are."

Yes, well, there we were.

When I was ten, the prettiest housemaid was Maureen. Black hair, blue eyes, fresh complexion. Like most of the maids in our house at that time, Maureen was an innocent-seeming girl from Ireland who went to confession and Mass. *Fresh off the boat*, my mother said. She must have had brothers: she wrestled with me after school every day and seemed to enjoy it. I sure did. Once, alone with Maureen, I took a piece of porcelain up from off the table. "Lift up your skirt and take down your underpants, or I'll drop this and tell them you did it," I said. She lifted up her skirt and showed me that she wasn't wearing underpants. After looking and looking, I looked in her face. Then I let the porcelain fall. It smashed on the floor. Maureen dropped her skirt and she smiled at me. Then she came and gave me a hug.

Maureen went and told the steward that she'd broken the ornament. She offered to pay for it. "Not-at-all, Maureen, you're a good girl," the steward will have said.

And so she was.

Le Ventre de Paris:
A Marriage Poem

I. La Rue Montorgeuil: the Market

They built the church here, imagining
He would come
to these cobbles, these streaming gutters,
the white pig's head skinned with drowsing eyes;
He would finger
dahlia petals mashed in the sewer,
chicken clutch, eel coil, choirs
of shrimp;
He would touch you, touch
me, because we are equally
soiled, because butchery
is life, and life runs
in us as down this street.

II. St. Eustache: the Market Church

The little we know
of St. Eustache
becomes him: how
this Roman (third
century A.D.) general

while hunting beheld
a crucifix
in a stag's antlers

and instantly
converted; how

broiled
in an iron bull, his cries
converted
to music; how, trans-
lated, he blesses

this butchers' cathedral,
its stained glass, its *clochards*,
its organ recitals,
its street
whistling with market blood.

A Rejected Chapter from *Hopscotch*

I know perfectly well the traps and snares of memory, but I think that the story of this "suppressed chapter" (number 126) is approximately as follows.

Hopscotch was born from these pages; born as a novel, as the intention of a novel, because several short texts already existed (like those which later became chapters 8 and 132), texts that were trying to cluster around a story. I know I wrote this chapter in one go, and it was followed immediately and with equal violence by the one that would eventually be called "the title chapter" (number 41 in the book). In this way there first was a kind of early core in which the images of Oliveira, Talita, and Traveler became defined; suddenly the lurch subsided and there was a painful pause, until with the same initial violence I understood that I had to leave it all and wait and go back through a plot of which I knew next to nothing, and write, using as a point of departure the short texts mentioned, the whole of the Paris section.

From that "other side" I jumped effortlessly to "this side," because Traveler and Talita had stayed there as if waiting, and Oliveira simply went to meet them, in exactly the way it is told in the book. And then one day I finished writing. I reread the mountain of papers, I added the host of elements that need to be included after a second reading, and I started to make a clean draft of the whole. It was then, I think, that I discovered that

this initial chapter, which had set the novel itself in motion, was superfluous.

The reason was simple and yet mysterious. I had not realized, two years into the novel, that Horacio's night in the mental institution, at the end of the book, took place within a make-believe equivalent to that of this first chapter; there, as well, someone was tying threads from one piece of furniture to another, from object to object, in a ceremony as inexplicable to Oliveira as it was to me. Suddenly the now-old first chapter became repetitious, even if in fact it had come first. I realized that I had to eliminate it, overcoming the unpleasant sense of having to pull away the cornerstone of the entire building. There was something like a feeling of guilt in that necessary act, something like ingratitude. That is why I began by looking for a possible solution, and when I wrote the clean draft I eliminated the names of Talita and Traveler—the main characters in the chapter—thinking that the faint enigma that would then surround them would deaden the flagrant parallel with the asylum chapter. An honest rereading was enough for me to understand that the threads had not moved an inch, that the ceremony was analogous and recurrent, and with no further thought I pulled out the cornerstone. As far as I know the house has not tumbled down.

These pages can't add anything to (or, I hope, take anything from) a book that embodies me as I was then, at a time of change, of search, of birds in flight.

 started because, after gulping down the last of the coffee, he signaled, but stared at him blankly and went to get the paper to read the obituary column, as is only proper after coffee. waited for a moment and then said he would make some more coffee because he still felt like drinking real coffee and not the whitish juice made, with the excuse that there was no ground coffee left in the blue tin. To this answered with an equally whitish look, and, when made the sign again, her eyes allowed themselves to be lowered and began to search (in the morning paper) for Juan Roberto Figueredo, r.i.p., passed away peacefully on 13 January 195–, with the blessing of the Church and the benefit of last rites. His wife, et cetera. Isaac Feinsilber, r.i.p.,

et cetera. Rosa Sanchez de Morando, r.i.p. No one she knew, not today, not even one name that sounded like someone she knew and would allow her to speculate on the deceased's identity and family connections. came back with the coffeepot and started by spooning a good amount of sugar into the cup of , who wasn't looking, deep in the paper, reading about Remigio Díaz, r.i.p. He then poured the coffee up to the rim of her cup and filled his own, while with the free hand he took out a packet of cigarettes and put it to his mouth as if he were about to bite it, but it was only to extract a cigarette dexterously without touching the others with his lips.

"I'm very sleepy," said after ten minutes.

"With the kind of news you read," said , who had been waiting for those words and was beginning to get seriously worried.

 yawned delicately.

"Take advantage now that the bed isn't made," said "You'll save yourself work afterwards." looked at him as if she hoped he would do his signaling again, but had begun to whistle, with his eyes glued to the ceiling—more precisely, on a cobweb. Then thought was miffed because she had not answered his signaling with the expected answer (passing her hand over her left ear as a sign of tenderness and compliance), and she went off to take her nap, leaving the table with the remains of a splendid casserole.

 waited three minutes, took off his pajama top, and entered the bedroom. was fast asleep, on her back. As it was hot, she had taken off the blanket as well as the top sheet; it was exactly what wanted, along with the fact that had nothing on except the nightdress in which she had gotten up that morning. The blue dressing gown was lying at the foot of the bed, covering her feet, and hooked it on his slipper and kicked it into a corner. He missed his shot and the dressing gown almost flew out of the window, which would have been a nuisance.

Out of the left pocket of his trousers took a tube of Secotine glue and a ball of black thread. The thread was shiny and rather thick, almost like wrapping string.

Carefully,　　　put his hand inside the right pocket of his trousers and took out a razor blade wrapped up in a piece of toilet paper. The toilet paper was torn and the blade's edge was visible. Sitting on the bed,　　　began to work while loudly whistling a bit from an opera. He was certain she would not wake up, because large quantities of coffee always made her sleep profoundly, and he would have been especially surprised if she woke up today, considering the penumbrate of oxtaline he had slipped in with the sugar. On the contrary,　　　's sleep was quite extraordinary; she huffed to take the air in, so that every five seconds her upper lip would blow up like the frill of a curtain, while the air blew underneath it in a noisy puff.　　　used this as a pacemaker to carry on whistling the opera while cutting the black thread, after calculating approximately how much he needed.

A tube of Secotine glue is opened by taking out the round-headed pin that serves both to pierce the tip and cover it, a detail that gives one an idea of the maker's ability. Once the pin is out, it is more than likely that a drop will appear on the tip of the tube, a drop of a rather revolting substance, with its already famous smell and certified mucilaginous properties. Very carefully, and while he embroidered variations on *Bella figlia dell'amore*,　　　wet the top of the black thread with Secotine and, leaning over,　　　pressed the wet tip in the middle of her forehead, leaving his finger in place long enough for the thread to stick to the forehead without sticking to his finger, that is to say, about four seconds, more or less. He then climbed on a chair (after placing the tube, the pin, and the ball of thread on the chest of drawers) and stuck the other end of the thread to one of the cut-glass prisms of the chandelier that hung over the bed and that　　　had refused to throw out the window in spite of his (now past and not repeated) pleading.

Satisfied that the thread was sufficiently taut, because he loathed sagginess in any human creation,　　　placed himself on the left side of the bed armed with the razor blade, and cut with a single stroke　　　's nightdress, beginning with the armpit. Then he cut along the seam of one sleeve, and did the same on the other side. The sleeves fell like snakeskins, but　　　proceeded with a certain solemnity when he came

to lifting the front of the nightdress, leaving stark naked. There was nothing on 's body that could be unknown to him, but the sudden contemplation of her body always dazzled him, although the Great Custom always managed to stale the effect. 's navel, more than anything else, made him giddy at first glance; it had something of confectionery, of failed transplant, of a pillbox thrown into a drum. Every time he saw it from above, felt the urgent desire to fill his mouth with saliva, very white and very sweet, and delicately spit on the navel, filling it to the rim with warm birthday lace. He had done so many times, but now was not the right moment, so he turned to look for the ball of thread and began cutting threads of different lengths, first measuring out certain distances. The first piece of thread (the one from the forehead to the chandelier was like an earlier pledge and therefore could not be taken into account) he stuck on the big toe of 's left foot; this piece went from the toe to the bathroom doorknob. The second piece of thread he stuck to the second toe and also to the doorknob; the third, to the third toe and also to the doorknob; the fourth, to the fourth toe and to a carving of a horn of plenty on the oak chest of drawers, split in three parts; the fifth thread was drawn from the little toe to another cut-glass prism of the chandelier. All this on the left side of the bed.

Satisfied, stuck another piece of thread to 's left knee and fixed it to the top of the window frame that looked out onto the hotel courtyard. At precisely that moment an enormous bluebottle fly flew in through the open window and began to buzz over 's body. Without paying any attention to it, stuck another thread to 's groin, at the top of her left thigh, and also to the upper rim of the window frame. He thought for a moment before making up his mind, and then took the tube of Secotine and squeezed it against 's navel until it was full. He immediately stuck six threads there and fixed five of them onto the cut-glass prisms hanging from the chandelier, and one onto the window frame. This did not seem enough, so he stuck eight more pieces of thread to the navel, which he stuck to seven more prisms and to the window frame. Stepping back two feet (he was somewhat cornered between the bed, the window, and the pieces of thread that led from to the window

frame), gave the finished work an appreciative look and found it satisfactory. He took out another cigarette and lit it with the butt that was already burning his lips. Suddenly he cut another half-dozen pieces of thread and stuck one to 's left nipple, another among the hairs of the left armpit, another to the earlobe, another to the left corner of the mouth, another to the left nostril, and another to the corner of the left eye. The first three he stuck to the cut-glass prisms of the chandelier, and the others to the window frame, with a great deal of difficulty because he had hardly any room to move. After doing this, he stuck pieces of thread to each finger of the left hand, to the elbow, and to the shoulder on that same side. Then he closed the tube of Secotine with the pin provided for that purpose, wrapped the razor blade in the piece of toilet paper he had carefully kept in the hip pocket of his trousers, and tucked away both things and the ball of thread in the left pocket of the above-mentioned article of clothing. Bending over very carefully so as not to touch the threads, which looked amazingly taut, he crept under the bed until he came out on the other side, completely covered in fluff and dust. He shook himself against the window that opened onto the street, took out once again his working utensils, and cut a number of pieces of thread that he stuck successively to different parts of the right side of 's body, in general keeping a symmetry with the left side but allowing himself certain variations: for instance, the piece of thread corresponding to the right earlobe was drawn between the earlobe and the bathroom doorknob; the thread leaving the corner of the right eye was stuck to the window frame opening onto the street. Finally (even though he was under no obligation to finish the task in a hurry), cut a fair number of pieces of thread, put a good quantity of Secotine on them, and plunged into a vehement improvisation, spreading them among 's hair and eyebrows and sticking most of them to the cut-glass prisms of the chandelier, but keeping some for the window frame opening onto the street, the bathroom doorknob, and the carved horn of plenty.

 After putting away the tube, the razor blade, and the ball of thread in his trousers, slid under the bed, dragged himself along till he came out at the foot, and kept sliding till he came

to the bathroom door. Very slowly, so as not to touch any of
the threads that led to the doorknob, he stood up and admired
his work. Through the windows came a yellowish, rather dirty
light, like the reflection of the peeling wall opposite that still
held on to the remains of a painting depicting a baby sucking
on something with a delighted look on his face; but the paint
had come off in strips, and instead of a mouth the baby had
a kind of purplish sore that seemed a poor recommendation
for the nutritive product praised below in rather stuttering
letters. The street was extremely narrow, and the windows on
one side were no more than five feet away from the other
side. At that time not one window was open, except 's,
but would probably not be there at that time, or would be
napping. The fly began to bother intensely, and he would
have liked to shoo it out the window, but in order to do this
he would have had to step forward to the foot of the bed and
wave his hand next to the chandelier, which would have been
impossible due to the large quantity of threads stretched in that
direction.

 "It's hot," thought , wiping his forehead with the
back of his hand. "It's really terribly hot."

 He would have liked to close the blinds, but quite apart
from the fact that it was difficult to wind one's way through
the threads, he would not have had enough light to see 's
body with the perfect clarity he needed. 's nakedness
seemed cut out against the background, not so much because
she lay with her back on the bed, but because the black threads
seemed to converge from everywhere and fall upon her. Had
they not been that taut, the overall effect would have been
completely bungled, and congratulated himself on his
dexterity, even though his naturally demanding spirit led him
to notice that the thread that led from the window frame to
the corner of the right eye was slightly slack. For a moment
he thought that had moved, altering the general balance
of tensions, but it was enough for him to eye the total array of
threads to dismiss that possibility. Furthermore, the amount of
sleeping powder he had put into 's coffee would not have
allowed even to blink. thought of sliding down to
the slackest thread and tightening it, but he would probably have

JULIO CORTÁZAR

spoiled some of the threads that met with this one on the window frame. He concluded that all in all the work was fine, and that he could allow himself a rest and another cigarette.

Eight minutes later he threw the butt out the window into the street, and took off his clothes without moving from where he was. His tall, thin body seemed to have come out of an engraving (an opinion expressed frequently). Even though could not see him, he gave the agreed-upon signal, and waited for an answer for about thirty seconds. Then he began to draw nearer the bed, little by little, avoiding with infinite care the threads that led to the bathroom doorknob. To do this he bent down and then stood up every time it was necessary, until he was standing exactly at the foot of the bed, closing a triangle formed by 's two feet and his own body. He waited a while, until opened her eyes and stared at him. As soon as he was sure that she could see him (because sometimes the state of unconsciousness lasted a few minutes after waking up), he lifted a finger and pointed to one of the threads. 's eyes began to wander up and down the threads, beginning with the ones that sprang from her eyebrows and the corners of her eyes, and following the entire length of her body. They rose to the cut-glass prisms of the chandelier and came back to their starting point; they left again, traveling to the window that looked onto the courtyard, and then returned to fix themselves to a knee or a nipple; they followed the black track to the window that opened onto the street, and returned to the groin or to the toes. was waiting with his arms crossed, his pose identical to that in a painting of the blue period.

When finished reconnoitering the threads, something like a sigh lifted her chest and projected her lips forward. Cautiously she moved her right arm, but she stopped when she heard the cut-glass prisms of the chandelier tinkle. The bluebottle fly flew sluggishly, slid among the threads, swirled around 's stomach, and was about to land on her mount of , but then it ascended to the ceiling and stuck to one of the moldings. and followed its flight with exasperated attention; they did not look at each other until they were sure that the fly had settled down on the ceiling with every intention of staying there.

Putting one knee down on the edge of the bed, bent his head and began leaning forward toward , who stared at him, motionless. The other knee appeared on the edge of the bed, while the torso advanced horizontally and one of the hands tried to grip the mattress, exactly in between 's legs. The pieces of thread surrounded him, but his movements were so precise that he did not so much as touch one when he lifted a knee and put it on the mattress, then lifted the second knee, together with the other hand, and remained on bent knees, completely arched between 's legs, breathing heavily because the maneuver had been slow and difficult and his calves hurt him, still perched as he was on the edge of the bed.

Lifting his head, looked at . Both were sweating, but while the sweat wrapped in a fine mesh of transparent droplets, both 's face and shoulders were sodden, even though her breasts and stomach were dry.

"One makes the signal, but the other plays with the clouds," said.

"Clouds are also an answer," said.

"A borrowed phrase."

"Exactly what you deserve."

 waited.

"You did it, at last," said . "You've been preparing me for months for this. First with your obsession with teaching me to recite filth, to dance like a Tibetan woman, to eat like an Eskimo, to make love like a dog. Then you forced me to cut my nails, you threw me into the street that day when it was hailing, you locked me in a wooden box with an infrared lamp, you bought me a stamp album. All that was nothing."

"You know how much I love you," said in a voice so low that opened her eyes as if in surprise. "My love is held tight in this fist, crumpled and broken till it becomes a screeching ball, a portable star that I can take out of my pocket and put next to your body, to burn it, to tattoo it. Every time I signal you, you don't answer, and the star fries my legs, runs over my ribs like a storm in the Sargasso Sea, that inexistence where the kraken floats, where the jellyfish couple in thousands, slowly turning in the night, in a bath of phosphorus and plankton."

"And is all that my fault?"

"You'll move the threads," said . "When you move your mouth, two of the threads change position."

"So what, the threads?" said .

"What do you mean, so what the threads?" said . "They took half an hour's work; I'm covered in dust and fluff. You never sweep under the bed. Even worse, you sweep the room and then hide the rubbish under the bed. I've just found out. My love is also like that, bits and pieces that come together and join and merge and stick to one another. But I sweat, which rubbish doesn't."

"It seems as if I've slept for a hundred years," said . "How long did I sleep, ?"

"A hundred years," said .

"That's a lot, a hundred years."

"For the one who stays awake."

"You must have been terribly bored."

"Exactly," said . "When you fall asleep you take the world away with you, and I am left in a sort of nothing crossed by lines of perspective. After a while it becomes boring."

"That's why you play like this," said , staring at the threads.

"This is not playing. To be naked looking at one another."

"I swear," said . "I think I didn't see the signal."

"Of course you saw it."

"Had I seen it I would have answered it. I'd rather be awake, with you."

"Explanations never suckled bees," said .

"Maybe I saw it and didn't answer it, but that was because of the heat and because after all I'd have had to do the dishes before coming to bed."

"First the dishes," said . "An excellent motto. At the bottom of how many knifings lies this excuse that no judge would accept. You'd lick the dirty dishes rather than lick my chest like an industrious little snail. Leaving a track in the shape of a four or an eight. Or better still, a seven, a number drunk in sacredness. But no, first we'll lick the dishes, as Queen Victoria would say. First we'll lick the dishes."

"But they're so filthy, ," said . "It's been fif-

teen days since we've washed anything in the kitchen. You noticed we had our lunch on dirty dishes, we can't go on like this."

"You're disturbing the threads," said .

"And if now you'd signal to me, if even now you'd . . ."

A whistle was heard, in the shape of an S. It came in through the window that opened onto the street.

"It's ," said . "Calling me."

"Put on something before leaning out," said . "You always forget you're naked."

"I'm always naked. You are the one who forgets that."

"Fine," said . "But at least put the pajama pants on. And till when do I have to stay like this?"

"I don't know," said . "First I've got to see what wants."

"To ask for something, I'm sure. A cigarette or matches, something like that."

"He's an addict."

"But you protect him."

"Well, if you're going to protect normal people . . ."

"True," said . "After all, is a good guy. Listen how he whistles. It's unbelievable how he can whistle. My mouth would fall to bits if I tried."

" is an alchemist," said . "He changes the air into a strip of mercury. Shit, he's fucked up."

"Why don't you look out and see what he wants? I'm not too comfortable here with these threads."

 stood for a moment, silently studying 's words.

"I know," he said. "What you want is that I let you go so that you can wash those dirty dishes."

"I swear I don't. I'll stay here with you. If you give me the signal. I swear I'll . . ."

"Bitch, bitch, you bitch," said . "If I give you the signal, eh? Now you come making up to me with the signal. Why should I care about the signal, if I had you any way I wanted while you slept? Even now all I have to do is slide down some twenty inches, making my way like a sea gull through that wonderful black web, those ropes on the mast of a galley, and enter you in one single thrust so that you scream out, because

you always scream out when I take you by surprise. And you're
longing for it, I've been smelling you for the past five minutes
and I know you're longing for it, I could enter you like a hand
into a used glove, you have the perfect level of dampness advised
by the specialists in copulatory matters, you hot sea slug."

"Did you really do it while I slept?" said .

"I did it in the most perfect way, but you would never
understand," said , looking at the threads in profound
admiration. "Beyond the signal, beyond your dirty kitchen, and
above all beyond your animal desire. Keep quiet, you're moving
the threads."

"Please," said . "Go and see what wants, and
then close the blinds and come to me. I swear I won't move, but
hurry up."

 once again studied 's words in silence.

"Maybe," he said. "You don't move. Do you want me to dry
you a bit with a towel? You're sweating like a stoat."

"Stoats don't sweat," said .

"They sweat gallons," said .

They always talked about stoats when they were making up.

"Now the problem is to see how I can get out of here,"
said . "There are so many pieces of string that I could
bump into one, and when you go backward you don't have the
same clairvoyance as when you go forward. It's incredible how
man was born for going forward. From behind we're nothing.
Like driving in reverse, even the cockiest will run over a mailbox
at the first change of gears. Guide me. First I'll take this leg out
and put this knee on the edge of the bed."

"A little further to the right," said .

"I think I'm touching a thread with my foot," said ,
looking behind him and correcting his movement.

"You hardly grazed it. Now put the other knee there, but
slowly. You look beautiful, all in a sweat. And the light from the
window seems to bathe you in green. You look like something
rotten, I swear. I never saw you look so lovely."

"Stop flattering me and guide me instead," said ,
furious. "You think I should put my foot down on the floor or
should I slide down? I'll scrape my shins if I do that; this bed
has a very sharp edge."

"First put the right foot down," said . "The thing is that I can't see the floor; how can I guide you if I can't even move?"

"There," said . "Now I'll bend down slowly and go back inch by inch, like in 's novels."

"Don't name that bird of ill omen," said .

Crawling like an everglades alligator, passed little by little under the threads that led to the window frame. He did not look up at again, but concentrated on studying the chest of drawers' horn of plenty, and the problem of overcoming the threads that went from the horn of plenty to one of the toes and to 's hair and eyebrows. Like that he passed under the greater part of the threads, but the last one he jumped. Only then, with his hand on the doorknob, did he look back at , who seemed asleep. He realized that instead of being at the window he was standing next to the door, and that from there it was easy to reach the head of the bed without disturbing the pieces of thread. Approaching her on tiptoes, he began to blow on her hair. The threads wavered, and the cut-glass prisms tinkled.

"Come here," said in a very low voice.

"Oh no," said , walking away. "I signaled you and you didn't answer."

"Come, come here immediately."

 looked toward the door. was breathing with difficulty, as if the black threads were sucking her blood. The crystal-clear note of one last cut-glass prism was heard, and then the silence of the afternoon nap. From the house opposite came a terrible whistle, and it was answered from below by something very similar to someone breaking wind.

"They've sent him a splendid fart," said . "He really deserves it."

"Please come here," she begged. " . It's painful to wait for you like this, I feel I'm going to die. Who'll cook your steak tonight?"

 opened his arms, took a deep breath, and jumped onto the bed, sweeping the threads with a fabulous swing. The racket made by the cut-glass prisms coincided with the crash of his feet touching the floor on the other side of the

bed and with 's yell, clutching her stomach with both hands. was still screaming in pain when fell on her, squashing her, weighing her down, biting her and fucking her. "My belly button hurts terribly," managed to say, but could not hear her, completely on the far side of words. The air smelled more and more of Secotine, and the bluebottle fly circled around the shaken chandelier. Bits of black thread twisted like insect legs all over the place, falling from the edge of the bed, crossing over each other and tearing with tiny snaps.

 had bits of thread in his mouth, under his nose, another coiled around his neck, and was moving her hands almost unconsciously, mingling caresses with desperate waves to rid herself of the threads that sprung from her everywhere. And all this seemed to last forever, and the horn of plenty was lying on the floor broken into three pieces, one bigger and the other two almost the same, as divine proportion requires.

—Translated by Alberto Manguel

An Exhibition

Bearded men, somewhere in the vicinity of sepulchers. The oaken door seemed never to have known the street. On one side a black rose rooted in the civilized soil, kept alive on the threshold of narrative to determine some inauspicious darkening. It might be a sluggish child, scourged and driven into the shadow of discipline and law. Morally as well as materially the women stood within a century.

From within the door there appeared a gray woman, the sunshine threw off a face of regularity, black eyes, startled and shone out misfortune, recklessness, desperate peculiarity, enclosing her female spectators. She has felt the grim gesture stitched to her shoulders. Open a passage! This time extremity is dragged into the sunshine!

She was there for them to spurn, know the intensity of a historical machine, in the grasp of the public head, she ascended this engine on proneness, flagrant gripe, displayed above the street: her part. And the image of this shuddering smile made the world darker for beauty.

They would find a theme in an exhibition like the present. It must have been the presence of men looking down from the platform, risking majesty. Herself the object, each man each woman their individual parts. When the whole scene seemed to vanish she was the most conspicuous object before them, intermingled with recollections. Another moment half-obliterated by point of view.

One came swarming back upon her stricken beauty, eyes bleared had a purpose—worn materials in these shifting scenes—came back feeding all the assembled regards. It sent a cry to assure herself that these were her realities, and the public had awaited her. From this consciousness of observation a convulsive force was pressed.

Old volumes and old portraits have to step forth. Compressed upon her face fixed arms, a whole people, burning down her face and lighting up a voice behind her. "I have been privileged to sit in the presence of so great a multitude." She bent her eyes to look inward. The interior air remained entire.

ROBERT RAUSCHENBERG

Seven
Works on Paper

Hoochi Koochi

Olive Shack

Pale Ground (pp. 62–63)

Blue Rise

Mast Major

Silver Bullet (pp. 68–69)

Purple Survivor

Seven Works on Paper

More than thirty years ago, Robert Rauschenberg invented a new kind of drawing, which he called "transfer drawing." To produce these intimate works, Rauschenberg transferred reproductions from printed media to paper (using solvents and rubbing techniques) and added pencil, ink, and watercolor washes by hand. Subsequently, he has employed a wide variety of techniques (such as silkscreen, collage, and direct manipulation of photo emulsion) to unite found images with gestural markings and thus to fix his allusive imagery.

Rauschenberg has always been a skilled photographer. He rarely travels without a camera, which he uses to accumulate an inventory of images for future work. Since the 1980s, he has chosen to employ almost exclusively his own photographs, rather than printed or found images, in his paintings and drawings. Such is the case with this portfolio.

The works in this portfolio were created explicitly for *Grand Street* 38. Here, Raushenberg has silkscreened his photographic images onto paper and overlaid them with acrylic washes.

—Walter Hopps

The Washerwoman's Fire

My immigrant mother cooked her white clothes alive.
From dawn to five she boiled them, turned them over,
Then removed them and said, "You must whip the dirt
From your clothes if you want them to be clean."
Then she rinsed them twice and hung them to dry facing
Southtown. There were shirts, sheets, and pillowcases;
Ruffles, ties, silks, and laces. Every Monday morning
My father built her iron pot a fire, then filled it with
Water. Carrying water is a tall command for a small daughter.
The fire seemed always there, so did the pot. On my natal day,
June 6, 1845, a spark reached beyond that pot and caught a ride
On a derelict piece of paper. It was a hungry wind which carried
That torch like a human passion. It stirred the entire community.
It left a trail as it began to eat the dry grasses and then the wood
Frames that shaped the houses; soon Southtown was all aflame.
The fire was sudden, quick, abiding. It grew to full life in an hour.
From Diamond to Wood to Water Street, smoke and wind swept
Fear into every heart. The losses were certain; the deaths
Tallied and assured. A lunching wind, an enormous fireball,
Swirled around a fireman and burned him through to the blood.
A delicate old woman who refused to leave her home knelt down
In a private place, and all that was left was a gathering of bones
Fused together. When the evening came, the fire settled gently.
The cinders smoldered. Now when I have cause to remember that special day
I think what a sudden, sudden ordering that fire made of the Southtown,
Celebrating my seventh birthday.

Wave Patterns

A Dialogue

Oe: We know that your father is a marine scientist, but exactly what branch of marine science does he specialize in?

Ishiguro: He's an oceanographer, so it's not exactly marine science. He's studied wave patterns. His work has to do with the tides and waves. His specialty in the 1960s was relevant to the British government's research on the North Sea, which they were very interested in at that time because of the oil.

Oe: In reading your novel *An Artist of the Floating World*, I was struck by the excellent descriptions of life in Japan, of Japanese buildings and landscapes. I would like to ask where you acquired this basic knowledge about your Japanese landscapes and characters, and to what extent they were a product of your imagination.

Ishiguro: Well, I think the Japan that exists in that book is very much my own personal, imaginary Japan. This may have a lot to do with my personal history. When my family moved from Nagasaki to England, it was originally intended to be only a temporary stay, perhaps one year or maybe two years. And so as a small child I was taken away from people I knew, like my grandparents and my friends. And I was led to expect that I

would return to Japan. But the family kept extending the stay. All the way through my childhood I couldn't forget Japan, because I had to prepare myself for returning to it.

So I grew up with a very strong image in my head of this other country, a very important other country to which I had a strong emotional tie. My parents tried to continue some sort of education for me that would prepare me for returning to Japan. So I received various books and magazines, these sorts of things. Of course, I didn't know Japan, because I didn't come here. But in England I was all the time building up this picture in my head of an imaginary Japan.

And I think when I reached the age of perhaps twenty-three or twenty-four I realized that this Japan, which was very precious to me, actually existed only in my own imagination, partly because the real Japan had changed greatly between 1960 and later on. I realized that it was a place of my own childhood, and I could never return to this particular Japan. And so I think one of the real reasons why I turned to writing novels was because I wished to re-create this Japan—put together all these memories and all these imaginary ideas I had about this landscape that I called Japan. I wanted to make it safe, preserve it in a book before it faded away from my memory altogether. So when I wrote, say, *An Artist of the Floating World*, I wasn't terribly interested in researching history books. I very much wanted to put down on paper this particular idea of Japan that I had in my own mind, and in a way I didn't really care if my fictional world didn't correspond to a historical reality. I very much feel that as a writer of fiction that is what I'm supposed to do: I'm supposed to invent my own world, rather than copying things from the surface of reality.

Oe: That seems to be a very concrete illustration of the way a writer's imagination takes shape. In my book *The Silent Cry*, I wrote about Shikoku. I was born and grew up in a mountain village on that island. When I was eighteen, I went to the University of Tokyo to study French literature. As a result, I found myself completely cut off from my village, both culturally and geographically. Around that time my grandmother died, and my mother was getting older. The legends and traditions and

folklore of my village were being lost. Meanwhile, here I was in Tokyo, imagining and trying to remember those things. The act of trying to remember and the act of creating began to overlap. And that is the reason I began to write novels. I tried to write them using the methods of French literature that I had studied. Reading your novels, and thinking about English literary history, I get the strong impression that, in terms of method, you are a novelist at the very forefront of English literature.

I was interested in the way that *An Artist of the Floating World* begins with a description of a large building, and how we enter the world of the novel through that building. In the same way, *The Remains of the Day* begins with a description of a large mansion. This entrance into the novel overlaps to a great extent with the earlier book. It was easy for me to see how the two books are connected, and how one develops from the other. Reading the two books together and observing this overlapping, I thought to myself that here was certainly a great novelist.

Ishiguro: That's very flattering. I'm very interested to hear some of the background about your being cut off from your past in Shikoku. Are you saying that the urge to remember or stay in touch with your past was actually crucial in making you become a writer?

Oe: I have a book that is just coming out in French translation from Gallimard, *M/T et l'histoire des merveilles de la forêt*. The "M" is for matriarch and the "T" is for trickster. A while ago I wrote a book called *Contemporary Games*, about the myths of the village and the universe of the village. As I wrote *M/T et l'histoire* I listened once more to my grandmother talking about cosmology, and wrote it down just as it was, in her own words. In fact, the history of my village is already lost. Almost everyone has forgotten it. For example, there is a place where dozens of people were killed in a riot, but no one remembers that. My family and especially my grandmother remembered those things very well, and told me about them. I grew up in the village listening to these stories. Then, when I was fourteen, I moved to the city and was completely cut off, while they were all dying. So now the only person who remembers the core of the myths

of that village is me. This is what I want to write about now. I want to write a book that will sum up or finish all of my work up to now. These things will be the main theme of the book, and right now they are what is most important to me.

Ishiguro: I hope the English translation will be appearing very shortly. I look forward very much to reading it. I think *The Silent Cry* is an extraordinary work. One of the reasons I think it's such a special work is that it's often difficult for a writer to get a certain distance from very personal events in his life that have touched and disturbed him. This book seems to stem from such an event, but at the same time you seem to have kept control, to have maintained an artistic discipline, so that it actually becomes a work of art that has meaning for everybody. It's not simply about Mr. Oe. It strikes me that one of the ways in which you manage that is a certain kind of humor, a unique tone. It's very different from the kind of humor found in most of Western literature, which is mainly based on jokes. In your books, everything has a peculiar sense of humor that is always on the verge of tragedy—a very dark humor. This is one of the ways in which you seem to have been able to keep under control events that must be very close to you. Mr. Oe the artist has always managed to keep in control of the work. But do you think this sort of humor is something unique to your own writing, or have you gotten it from a larger Japanese tradition?

Oe: It's interesting that you should ask that, because one of the things I feel is unique about your work is your control over the distance from the periods and characters in your work. All of your books have a distinct tone, even though they are connected on a deeper level. So I appreciate your comments about the tone and distance in my works.

I think that the problem of humor, which you just brought up, is a very important one. This is one of the points in which I differ from Yukio Mishima. Mishima was very strongly rooted in the traditions of Japanese literature, especially the traditions of the center—Tokyo or Kyoto—urban traditions. I come from a more peripheral tradition, that of a very provincial corner of the island of Shikoku. It's an extremely strange place, with a long

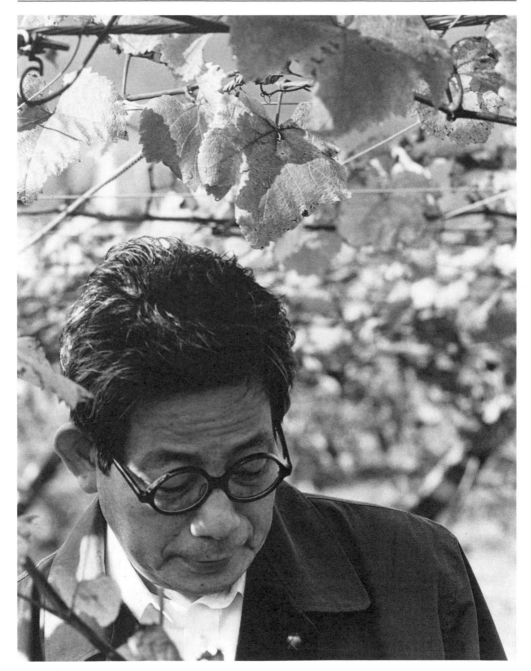

Kenzaburo Oe

history of maltreatment, out there beyond the reach of culture. I think my humor is the humor of the people who live in that place. Mishima had a great deal of confidence in his humor, so perhaps it's accurate to say that his was the humor of the center, whereas mine is the humor of the periphery.

Ishiguro: I would be quite interested to hear what you feel about Mishima. I'm often asked about Mishima in England— all the time, by journalists. They expect me to be an authority on Mishima because of my Japanese background. Mishima is very well known in England, and in the West generally, largely because of the way he died. But also I suspect that Mishima's image confirms certain stereotypical images of Japanese people for the West. And this is partly why I think he is easy for Western audiences. He fits certain characteristics. Of course, committing seppuku is one of the clichés. He was politically very extreme. The problem is that the whole image of Mishima in the West hasn't helped people there form an intelligent approach to Japanese culture and Japanese people. It has perhaps helped people to remain locked in certain prejudices and very superficial, stereotypical images of what Japanese people are like. Most people seem to regard Mishima as a typical Japanese, in some sort of way. Of course, I never know quite what to say in response to this because I know very little about Mishima and very little about modern Japan. But that is certainly the impression I get—that in the West he is being used to confirm some rather negative stereotypes. I wonder what you think about Mishima and the way he died, what that means for Japanese people, and what that means for a distinguished author such as yourself.

Oe: The observations you just made about the reception of Mishima in Europe are accurate. Mishima's entire life, certainly including his death by seppuku, was a kind of performance designed to present the image of an archetypal Japanese. Moreover, this image was not the kind that arises spontaneously from a Japanese mentality. It was the superficial image of a Japanese as seen from a European point of view, a fantasy. Mishima acted out that image just as it was. He created himself

exactly in accordance with it. That was the way he lived, and that was the way he died. Professor Edward Said uses the word "orientalism" to refer to the impression held by Europeans of the Orient. He insists that orientalism is a view held by Europeans and has nothing to do with the people who actually live in the Orient. But Mishima thought the opposite. He said, in effect, "Your image of the Japanese is me." I think he wanted to show something by living and dying in exact accordance with the image. That was the kind of man he was and that was why he gained literary glory in Europe and the world.

But what in fact happened is that Mishima presented a false image. As a result, the conception of Japanese people held by most Europeans has Mishima at one pole and people like Akio Morita, chairman of Sony, at the other pole. In my opinion, both poles are inaccurate. But if this is the case, where can we look for a more accurate image of the Japanese people? Going back to your book *An Artist of the Floating World*, at the very end there is a scene with a number of young Japanese and the artist, who is looking at them in a warmhearted way. I think that people like those young Japanese really do live in Japan, and that they are the ones who have brought prosperity to the Japanese economy. Of course, Mishima had nothing to say about them. And writers like me, who take a negative view of Japan, have not captured them either. So I think that your novel exerted a good influence on perceptions of Japan in Europe, a kind of antidote to the image of Mishima.

I have a question I wanted to ask. Reading your work and talking to you, one does not at all get the impression of someone born in Japan. In the case of Conrad, one of my favorite authors—to me he is a kind of ideal novelist—one gets the strong impression that he is a genuinely English author, as well as a true European. On the day when you received the Booker Prize, there were reports in the Japanese mass media of your remarks on Salman Rushdie.* There were many people who were moved by those remarks, including myself. We felt

* In his speech accepting the Booker Prize, Ishiguro said: "It would be improper for us not to remember Salman Rushdie this evening and think about the alarming situation and plight in which he finds himself."

that this person was a genuinely European novelist, a genuinely European personality, that this was real European intelligence.

The Japanese themselves want to be perceived as peaceful and gentle, like Japanese art—landscape paintings and so on. They don't want to be seen as economic imperialists or military invaders. They would like others to think of flower paintings, something quiet and beautiful, when they think of Japan. When your books first began to appear in Japan, that was how they were introduced. You were described as a very quiet and peaceful author, and therefore a very Japanese author. But from the first I doubted that. I felt that this was an author with a tough intelligence. And in fact that has been demonstrated again with each of your books. Your style always involves a double structure, with two or more intertwined elements. I also felt that this kind of strength was not very Japanese, that this person was, rather, from England.

Ishiguro: Well, I don't try to be a quiet writer. That's really a question of technique more than anything else. There's a surface quietness to my books—there aren't a lot of people getting murdered or anything like that. But for me they're not quiet books, because they're books that deal with the things that disturb me the most and the questions that worry me the most. They're anything but quiet to me.

On the question of being a European writer, I think that partly this has been the effect of my not knowing Japan very well. I was forced to write in a more international way. If I had continuously returned to this country after I left it in 1960, and if I had been more familiar with Japan all through my growing up, I think perhaps I would have felt a greater responsibility to represent Japanese people in this way or that way, to be a kind of spokesman, if you like, of Japan in England. But as things worked out, I didn't return. This is my first return to this country in thirty years. I was very aware that I had very little knowledge of modern Japan. But I was still writing books set in Japan, or supposedly set in Japan. My very lack of authority and lack of knowledge about Japan, I think, forced me into a position of using my imagination, and also of thinking of myself as a kind of homeless writer. I had no obvious social role, because I wasn't a

very English Englishman, and I wasn't a very Japanese Japanese either.

And so I had no clear role, no society or country to speak for or write about. Nobody's history seemed to be my history. And I think this did push me necessarily into trying to write in an international way. What I started to do was to use history. I would search through history books for information in the way that a film director might search for locations for a script he has already written. I would look for moments in history that would best suit my purposes or what I wanted to write about. I was conscious that I wasn't so interested in the history per se, that I was using British history or Japanese history to illustrate something that was preoccupying me. I think this made me a kind of writer who didn't actually belong. I didn't have a strong emotional tie with either Japanese history or British history, so I could just use them to serve my own personal purposes.

I wonder, Mr. Oe, do you feel responsible for how Japanese people are perceived abroad? When you are writing your books, are you conscious of an international audience and of what the books will do to Western people's perceptions of Japan? Or do you not think about things like that?

Oe: I was interviewed once by a German television station. The interviewer had translated one of my books into German. He asked me whether it was very important to me to be translated into German. I said no, and a deathly silence fell over the studio. The reason I said no is simply that I write my books for Japanese readers rather than for foreigners. Moreover, the Japanese readers I have in mind are a limited group. The people I write for are people of my own generation, people who have had the same experiences as myself. So when I go abroad, or am translated abroad or criticized abroad, I feel rather indifferent about it. The responsibilities I feel are to Japanese readers, people who are living together with me in this environment.

Speaking as a reader, foreign literature is very important to me. William Blake is important to me. I've written one book based on Blake, and one based on Malcolm Lowry. Another book was about a Dante specialist who lives out in the country. With respect to Dante, I have been influenced in various ways by

scholars from your country. So in that sense I have been much
influenced by foreign literature. I read your books in English,
for example. Still, I think that when I write my books, I write
them for Japanese readers. I feel a certain sense of responsibility
that I just can't break out of, even though I feel that there is
probably something mistaken about that attitude. Naturally, I
believe that a real novelist is international, like yourself. In your
case, of course, I think that in addition to being international
you are also very English. In *The Remains of the Day* you
discovered viewpoints from which it is possible to describe both
English people and Americans well. The viewpoint is completely
different from that of a Japanese person or a Chinese person.
From a certain viewpoint, it is possible to see an English person
well, and also an American person. And that viewpoint has
produced your style. I think that this sort of author is genuinely
European, international in an essential way. So it might be that
I am a more Japanese author than Mishima. I myself hope
that younger Japanese authors will be able to discover a more
international standpoint or outlook.

Ishiguro: There never seems to be a clear relationship between
the audience an author thinks he is addressing and the audience
that in fact the author does come to address. Many of the great
classical writers, whether the ancient Greeks or whoever, had
no idea they would eventually address people from cultures
very, very different from themselves. Possibly Plato was writing
simply for the people who were living in Athens at the time, but
of course we read him many, many years later in very different
cultures. I sometimes worry that writers who are conscious of
addressing an international audience could actually have quite a
reverse effect, that something very important in literature might
actually die because people are watering down their artistic
instincts. It's almost like a mass-marketing exercise.

 I worry particularly because this is a time when American
culture, or what you might call Anglo-American culture, has
become pervasive all around the world—in Asia, Latin America,
and so forth. It seems to be growing and growing. Perhaps it
is very important that writers not worry about this question
of audience. You yourself, Mr. Oe, may think you are writing

Kazuo Ishiguro

only for your own generation, for the Japanese. But your books are read by lots of people outside that group. People want to translate your work. It seems that as the years go by your reputation grows in different parts of the world. This shows that someone can address a small group of people, but if that work is powerful and sincere it will have a universal, international audience.

On the other hand, I know that there are many writers who are consciously trying to write the novel that is all ready for translation. And of course nobody particularly wants to read these things, because they have lost some sort of initial strength that comes from the intensity of addressing a small group. Perhaps whether a writer is international or not is something that the writer cannot control. It's almost accidental. But often, I think, the deeper the work, and the deeper the truth of the work, the more likely it is to be international, whether the author is consciously addressing a small group of people or a large number of people. Do you think younger writers in Japan are worried about this question of how international they are?

Oe: In last evening's edition of the *Asahi Shimbun* there was an article about how a translation of a work by the novelist Haruki Murakami is being read widely in New York. The article quoted a review in the *New York Times* to the effect that it was now possible to imagine a literature of the Pacific Rim.

For the past week I have been thinking about just what sort of novelist you are. My conclusion is that, rather than being an English author or a European author, you are an author who writes in English. In terms of furnishing the materials for literature, there is a tremendous power in the English language. Somehow it seems that the initiative in world literature has been with English, especially in the field of the novel. As long as he has the English language, an author can leave England and still remain a great writer. Lawrence was that way, and Lawrence Durrell; also E. M. Forster. I felt that by thinking of you in this way, as a writer of English, I had got hold of something essential. By way of comparison, Murakami writes in Japanese, but his writing is not really Japanese. If you translate it into American English it can be read very naturally in New York. I

suspect that this sort of style is not really Japanese literature, nor is it really English literature. But as a matter of fact, a young Japanese author is being read widely in the United States, and I think that this is a good sign for the future of Japanese culture. A young Japanese writer has achieved something that I was never able to achieve, nor Mishima nor Kōbō Abe.

Ishiguro: I think I too share these same worries. I attended a lecture by the European intellectual George Steiner, who is at Cambridge and very well known in Britain. I think you are familiar with many of his ideas. One of his constant worries is that all the cultures of the world are disappearing because they are being swallowed up by this ever-growing, large blanket called Anglo-American culture. He is very disturbed by the fact that scientific papers in China and here in Japan are often written originally in English because they have to be presented at conferences where only English is understood. In the communist countries the young people listen to the latest Western rock music. He is very afraid of a certain kind of death of culture, because this bland, colorless, huge blanket called Anglo-Americanism is spreading around the world. In order to survive, people have to sacrifice many things that make their culture unique and in fact make their art and culture mean something, and instead contribute to this meaningless blanket, this strange thing that is conquering the world.

I think that is quite an important thing to be concerned about. Certainly my generation of writers in Britain has perhaps not worried about that kind of thing enough. We have perhaps been concerned about the opposite problem, of not being international enough. I think this is certainly a problem that we have to think about. I think it will be very strange if we all contribute to the same sort of culture, if we're all addressing the same sort of audience. We could all end up like international television. A lot of television programs now are rather superficial, but they're international. It would be sad if literature and serious art were to go the same way—to the lowest common denominator—in order to appear international.

There is a sense among younger writers in England that England is not an important enough country anymore. The

older generation of writers assumed that Britain was a very important country, and so if you wrote about Britain and British problems it would automatically be of global significance. The younger generation of writers in England are very aware of the fact that this is no longer true, that England is now rather like a little provincial town in the world. Some younger British writers have a kind of inferiority complex; that is, they have to consciously make an effort to address international themes, because if they simply write about life in Britain, nobody is going to be interested. Perhaps that feeling doesn't exist in the United States or Japan, since there is a strong sense that these two societies are now at the center of the world, and the twenty-first century is going to be somehow dominated by these two powers. But, certainly, living in England, I feel that same pressure, that I have to be international. Otherwise I'm going to end up in the same position as Danish or Swedish writers, of being very peripheral, because a lot of the great questions of today are passing Britain by. In a way, I think young Japanese authors don't need to feel that sort of inferiority, just because of the way history is moving.

Oe: Of course, I have nothing against the fact that Japan is becoming rich because of radios and automobiles. I don't own an automobile, but I do have a radio. But I do think that the state of the economy and the state of literature are unrelated. I think Japanese authors should clearly realize that Japanese literature is very peripheral. When a peripheral literature attempts to become a central literature, one of the things that happens is that it tries to become exotic. I think Mishima tried to create a literature of the exotic. But I believe that attempt was mistaken. Paradoxically, it may be possible for Japanese writers to play a certain role in world literature if they express Japanese concerns in a literature of the periphery.

I am familiar with George Steiner. He seems to be very fond of the idea that things are dying—first it was tragedy and now it is culture. I think that the image of Anglo-American culture as a huge blanket spreading across the world is one of his best. But I can't really agree with what you said about England being a peripheral nation in terms of the world economy

and international relations. I believe that in terms of culture, England still occupies a very important place in the world, and will continue to do so in the future. Looking forward to the twenty-first century, it doesn't seem to me that Japan will become a cultural center just because of its economic strength. I don't believe that American cultural spokesmen will have a very great deal of power, or that Soviet cultural spokesmen will be very powerful. I think that in the twenty-first century, statements by isolated writers and scholars from small countries that appear to be on the periphery will play a very important role in world culture. One example is the novelist Italo Calvino, who recently died a tragic death. He was scheduled to deliver the Mellon Lectures at Harvard University, and was working on the manuscript for those lectures until he died on the day before he was to leave for the United States. The manuscript has been translated into English as *Six Memoirs for the Next Millennium.* Reading it, I think that this work by a novelist from Italy, a country that is economically and politically on the periphery, contains things that will be of central importance in the next century. Another example is the Czech novelist Milan Kundera, now living in exile in France. Reading, for example, the Israel Address, which is found at the end of his book *The Art of the Novel,* I think we will find the most central expression of how a writer will have to live and act today. So I think what writers from Japan must learn is that they need to think about how they can contribute to world culture as representatives of a small but cultured nation in Asia. Moreover, they should do so without the help of businessmen or politicians. They will have to open up on their own a road to England, or a road to France, simply as writers.

Ishiguro: I would like to add to my earlier remarks. It wasn't simply because Britain was declining as an economic power that I was suggesting writers in Britain had a sense they were peripheral. I don't think it is really so much in connection with economic power. In fact, I think it is in some ways quite the reverse.

Writers from Britain, and to a certain extent writers from Germany and France—and I myself have had this experience—

go to an international writers' conference and somehow feel
inferior compared to writers who come from places like Africa
or Eastern Europe or Latin America, in the sense that in many of
the great intellectual battles—between liberty and authoritarian
regimes, or between communism and capitalism, or between
the Third World and the industrialized world—the front line
somehow seems to be in these countries, and there seems to be
a more clearly defined role for writers like Kundera or some
of the African writers. Writers from all the Eastern European
countries always seem to have some sort of clear political role
to play. This may well be a mistaken assumption, but it's an easy
assumption that comes over a lot of us who come from the safer
countries, if you like, the safe, prosperous countries like Britain
or West Germany or France, although the situation has suddenly
changed for the West Germans.

In historical terms, if we are writing from Britain or Sweden
or France in the latter part of the twentieth century, we are
writing from somewhere very far away from where the main
events are taking place, and we somehow lack the natural
authority of writers in Czechoslovakia or East Germany or Africa
or India or Israel or the Arab countries. And I think this is the
reason for this inferiority complex, rather than that Britain is
simply not quite as important an economic power as it used to
be. Of course it is still a very powerful economic force. But in
terms of the great intellectual debates that seem to be central to
the latter part of the twentieth century, there is the feeling that
perhaps we in England are in the wrong place to view the big
battles.

Perhaps it's a good thing that British writers feel they
have to travel, at least in their imaginations. I think the
younger generation of British writers, much more than the older
generation, tends to write novels that are not set in Britain, or
at least not set in their time. They look back through history for
a time when Britain itself was in crisis, and so the war figures
quite large. Or they use their imaginations to create complete
imaginary landscapes. This kind of thing is happening more and
more, and I think it comes out of this idea that somehow England
is far away from the important events—political and social—in
the world. Perhaps writers in Japan and the United States do

not feel it quite so much, because there is a sense that somehow, quite aside from the economic question, Japan and America are at the forefront of something crucial that is about to happen in the world. I think that has a certain effect on how writers view their work and on where they go for material to feed their imaginations.

Oe: When I myself go abroad to participate in various conferences, it is always simply as an individual writer. I think that the things I have talked about have been more or less unrelated to Japan's economic growth. My sense of Japan is that it is still a peripheral country, and that in spite of its economic power it is still not living up to its international role, particularly in Asia. Thinking back, I think I may share some of the responsibility for this state of affairs, so I talk about that and the sort of things that a writer, as a writer, might be able to do to compensate.

For some reason, Japanese writers tend to stay away from international writers' conferences. Up to now, at least, there have not been many authors who have gone abroad to speak out about Japan's place in the world, about the contradictions felt by Japanese writers in the midst of economic prosperity, about the things that trouble them deeply. So for my part I am trying to do that, little by little. Japan has many very capable businessmen and politicians, but as a novelist I want to speak out internationally about things that they never mention. And I think it is meaningful for writers from abroad, especially young writers like yourself, to come to Japan to look closely at this country and to meet Japanese intellectuals. I hope this will lead to a deeper understanding of things such as the difficult role played by Japanese intellectuals amid material prosperity, and to cultural encounters at a genuinely substantial level.

The Way of Eating Fried Sausage

I am staying at the faculty club of the University of California at Berkeley while I serve for a few days as a short-term research associate and a speaker at a symposium. The history of the university, or of the people in the university, can be seen in the way the simple but refined Continental breakfast is served here; I do not have even the slightest dissatisfaction with it. For dinner, the students eat out at Chinese or Mexican restaurants in the university's lively neighborhood. If I eat at a restaurant operated by refugees who have no liquor license, I stop on the way home at a students' bar and drink beer poured from a pitcher. On the whole, as my disposition is that of a generation that learned to use self-control over the extravagant pleasures of good food, I find this arrangement more than adequate.

There is no need for me to cook here, but since I confine myself to my room over the weekend while working on the outline of my speech for the public seminar and checking its English translation, I find that it is a waste of time to cross the wide campus to the student center. Instead, I cook lunch at the visitors' kitchen. If I may tell you the truth, I cook and eat Korean instant noodles, stir-fried with frozen vegetables from Taiwan.

This type of modest meal, which I used to have when I was

living away from my family in my adolescent years, is quite familiar to me. Those meals were prepared in a very short time and eaten quickly. Even today, with a family of my own, I still eat in the same manner. At home, I attend formal dinner parties several times each year, and when discussions grow animated I often sense that the waitress or geisha sitting near the lacquered tables in front of me feels a restrained contempt for my ill manner of eating. It is nevertheless something I do not particularly pay attention to.

But now, as I eat here in the dormitory at a table that is also used for cooking, in the white kitchen that seems able to accommodate an operating table, I feel that I am undergoing some changes. With the tip of my tongue, I lick the pod of a soybean, a small tuft of broccoli, or a string of bean sprout, and slowly, ever so slowly, as if moving in a dream, I savor each taste. Then I call myself back—"Hey? Hey!"—and return to my usual hurried way of eating.

Meanwhile, my thoughts wander to Uncle Hyōei for the first time in quite a while. Because the ceramic bowl I eat from has no stand on its bottom, it is hard for me to hold when I pour hot water into it. After dinner, as I rinse the bowl, the water feels cool to my wrist, and without my understanding why, this feeling awakens thoughts of Uncle Hyōei once again. As I say to myself, "Hey? Hey!" while lightly washing the dishes, I feel a smile begin to stiffen the area around my cheekbones.

Truthfully speaking, this has been a frequent experience lately. After returning to my room, I lie on my bed; among the books I have brought along—like the household medicines one brings on a trip—I find a copy of *The Buddha's Last Journey*, the *Maha Pari Nirvana Sutra*, Iwanami Library edition. The book is a volume from Uncle Hyōei's *Ti Pitaka Sutra*, which he read throughout his life. And I decide to write about what is involved when I say to myself, "Hey? Hey!" as far as I can tell.

First of all, Uncle Hyōei is called "Uncle," but this is nothing more than a convenient way of addressing him. The correct usage of this term is another matter. My relatives have complicated feelings regarding Uncle Hyōei's life, particularly the way he lived during his later years and the way he died. I would like to warn you beforehand that there was no real uncle-

and-nephew relationship between Uncle Hyōei and myself. Still, when I called him "Uncle," I always thought that I had the Chinese characters for "elder uncle" in my head.* Through Lévi-Strauss's research on family relations, I became conscious of the fact that my actual relationship with Uncle Hyōei—who has influenced me deeply—can be understood as similar to my relationship with my mother's older brother. At any rate, I will proceed by calling him "Uncle Hyōei."

The very early stages of the war. A ceremony on New Year's morning. Rice grains are placed on the small wooden stand, and rice cakes for offerings are piled atop one another on a fern, surrounded by tangerines, dried persimmons, and dried chestnuts. These foods are first offered to honor the gods or ancestors; according to our ages we would kneel in front of our grandmother and our parents (Grandmother and Father soon passed away and only Mother remained), and later, after bowing and choosing the one offering we liked most, we would clap our hands in worship and leave to eat anywhere we liked. That was how we celebrated New Year's Day; our village on the island of Shikoku did not have such customs as giving money to children. In this remote valley, children could not have taken money to go shopping, eat out, or go to the movies; there were no shops, restaurants, or movie houses. Yet it was a very special day and one could feel a tense excitement in the air.

It was an event that also included so many complicating elements that one could call it theatrical. Both physically and psychologically, it was truly a theatrical performance. Each child would pick up his offering to the gods or ancestors from the wooden table and, in effect, ask for a forecast of his fortune, aspirations, and what his year might bring. The chosen offering served also as a symbol for the confirmation of his prayers and desires. The symbol operated only at the level of simple wordplay, linking the ideas in the child's mind and the name of the food. Or perhaps it worked at the level of the play of

* Japanese distinguishes between uncles who are older than the parents and those who are younger. The Chinese characters for each are different, but the pronunciation is identical.

imagination that was directly evoked by the taste of the food, its resistance to the teeth, or its feel on the tongue.

Dried chestnuts, dried persimmons, tangerines: I know their names and flavors, but as to the meanings given to such material characteristics, all I can clearly remember now is the opposition created by placing a dried chestnut at one end of the table and a dried persimmon at the other. In particular, the symbolism of the dried chestnut, also called "victory chestnut," is etched painfully deep in my memory even now. The polarity and respective symbolism of the dried persimmon and the tangerines were so clear that it was unnecessary to inquire about them; because of that, I have no way of remembering what they were. I would concentrate on whether I should take the dried chestnut that year; the tension at the height of the ceremony was like the string of a New Year's kite, high in the sky, ringing in the wind.

Why was there tension? As I passed into adolescence, I fervently wanted, to the depth of my emotions and my senses, to choose the dried persimmon. During the war, local villages experienced a shortage of sweet things. Or, rather, an exhaustion. All the cells in my body craved sweets. Of course, my body was disturbed by uneasy thoughts, which were undoubtedly caused by my passing through a period of healthy growth. During wintertime, dried persimmons were the only sweets. The light juice of the tangerine could not be compared to the resplendent sweetness—I would have carved the adjective "resplendent" on my heart, had I known it then— of the persimmon. It was a special luxury. It wasn't that children would never get such dried persimmons; before spring, each child would probably be given four or five. But the sensation of biting into the dried persimmon, having it lie on your tongue, and letting it slip down your throat was such a sweet experience that perhaps this is why I remember it as an extremely unusual food.

The foods offered on the New Year's table to honor our ancestors and the gods of the common ancestors of the village were all special, though the dried persimmon was the most special. At our home, tart persimmons were picked from the old, tall tree on the slope down to the river behind the house. The war had progressed, and, since the food shortage, only a little

wheat and potatoes were cultivated in the fields. A branch would be caught using a long bamboo pole with openings cut at its tip, and the persimmons would be wrenched off. Grandmother and Mother would peel off the skins and hang the fruit on a straw rope to dry. There were only a certain number of fruit, and they varied in size. When one tore open the swollen, plump dried persimmons, the reddish-black, jelly-like, wet, smooth flesh of the fruit appeared; the seed was covered with a translucent membrane that looked as if it were still alive. Only the best persimmons were offered on the New Year's table, and they became objects for the children to choose. That is, any child could take a persimmon from the table and thereby receive it in a one-to-one communion with his ancestor or the god of the common ancestors. Then, in whatever corner of the house he chose, each child could savor the resplendent sweetness of the dried persimmon to his heart's content.

After the war began, however, I did not choose the dried persimmon from the New Year's table even once. It was only natural that my younger brothers and sisters would pick the dried persimmon, so I would take the Tamba chestnut, which was dried to a dark brown. Filled with regretful longing for the persimmon, I would spit out the dry, coarse outer skin and roughly peel and throw out the soft inner skin. Then I would chew the tasteless cold lump of chestnut meat, moistening it with saliva. I would taste a slight sweetness, like a dim light seen through closed eyes. However, the chewed-up chestnut meat would, for the most part, already have been swallowed.

Why would I take the dried chestnut instead of the dried persimmon? On New Year's Day, year after year, as I became so tense that my brain seemed to go numb, I would stretch out my hand, specially cleaned to the wrist, and snatch the dried chestnut; on the verge of tears, I would turn red, cast my eyes downward, and leave. I did this for victory, for no reason other than for the sake of national victory. The dried chestnut was a victory chestnut. On New Year's Day I chose the victory chestnut, because as a younger member of a nation at war I prayed to my ancestors and to the god of our common ancestors for victory in the Pacific War. After I took the dried chestnut, I would bow, clap both hands together, and say an

inner prayer. This prayer no longer had anything to do with the fate of the country. By picking the dried chestnut instead of the dried persimmon, I felt that I had fully accomplished my public obligations as a young citizen. What more could I do? My prayer was for my own unfolding destiny. I clasped the small dried chestnut, hard as a stone, and, trembling, prayed with a sad heart.

"To all my ancestors, all the honorable gods of the common ancestors, who live in the valley in the forest: you do not need to change the odd shape of my face or body. Instead, please make me smarter. You do not have to make me excessively intelligent, like Uncle Hyōei; just a little of his intelligence passed this way would be fine. I beg you to make me smarter."

As I lowered my voice in prayer, my relatives sat around the table: my father and my grandmother at the upper end, my mother at the lower. I recall that they all wore their family-crest kimonos and watched us intently. That was more than two years before the end of the war. In the autumn and winter of the year before Japan's defeat, the two authority figures in my family, my father and my grandmother, passed away in succession, leaving behind my mother, who was in her mid-thirties, and myself.

Before that frightening year, when we had numerous storms and floods, it was already apparent, even to the children, that Uncle Hyōei was "excessively intelligent," that he was a "social misfit." At that time, Uncle Hyōei was on a leave of absence from Waseda University, where he was a student in the Department of Sciences and Engineering. He must have been on leave for two or three years by then. For more than thirty-five years, Uncle Hyōei was considered a "social misfit" by the inhabitants of the valley, young and old, male and female. He never modified his way of life and, unusually for a social misfit, he lived a long life and died a natural death.

Early on the day of my father's funeral, Uncle Hyōei climbed the hill to our house. He was dressed appropriately, but smelled strongly of sheep—for reasons I'll explain a little later. I was a young boy, still stupefied rather than grieving. Uncle Hyōei sat in front of me; from a cloth bundle by his side he took out some books. Now that I think of it, they were the type of books that

students of science and engineering were surely collecting just before the war: H. G. Wells's history of science, Julian Huxley's observations on the life of ants, *The Life of Madame Curie,* as well as books like Kazukiyo Yamamoto's or Hoei Nojiri's on the stars. Uncle Hyōei placed the books in front of me one by one and watched my response. Thinking that these books would help a child who had just lost his father to forget his sorrow, he hoped to give away those that interested me and take the remainder home.

Finally Uncle Hyōei took from his lap the cloth that he had wrapped the books in. He stood up and bowed deeply to my mother in the manner of a stranger, not, perhaps, because my parents had assisted him with his school fees when he entered Waseda University but because he was always in awe of my mother. Mother returned the same bow, and Uncle Hyōei's pale face, with its overgrown beard, flushed. He left through the back door, saying, "It was a mistake to think that one could measure a child's grief by material standards." Still dazed, I only remember timidly touching the books with the tip of my finger.

Now let me explain about Uncle Hyōei's school fees. The opinion in the valley, which had reached even the children's ears, was that my father's action was intrusive. I was happy with it, since I took pride in having a relative who had been admitted into a famous university in Tokyo, and I had great respect for Uncle Hyōei as well. As a child, I was indifferent to my family's long-standing status and rank, founded on our supposedly considerable wealth, and I ignored such gossip. At any rate, let me use what I know to reconstruct how the rumors came about and what they said. The house where Uncle Hyōei was born was located on a wide spread of land along a road in the ravine, downriver from the center of town. For generations, the rice fields below the house had been farmed by Uncle Hyōei's family, but the majority of the land was allotted to tenant farmers. Where the rice fields are obstructed by a dense cluster of cypress and white fir—that is, at the lower edge of the forest—and beyond the end of the stone road, stands a small uninhabited temple, virtually concealed. At this "Mountain Temple," the position of chief priest had traditionally been held by an unmarried member of Uncle Hyōei's family.

Uncle Hyōei's father was the village treasurer, and his uncle, who had died at a young age, was the last chief priest of the Mountain Temple.

In our region Uncle Hyōei was said to be fastidious, because he detested contact with women. For this reason, and also because he was the youngest of the male children in his family, everyone, including himself, had no doubt that he would go to the Soto Zen-affiliated university and become the chief priest at the Mountain Temple. While attending the regional metropolitan junior high school, he is said to have carefully read the *Ti Pitaka Sutra*. Because of that, he was considered eccentric and oddly mature; while he solved geometry and analytical entrance-exam questions, he read through the entire collection of books handed down through generations at the Mountain Temple. It was said that in scholarship he already surpassed the chief priest from the large temple above the river. In fact, the chief priest avoided getting caught in discussions with him, and rumor had it that during Uncle Hyōei's summer vacations from junior high school, he wouldn't dare come out into town.

However, from the end of his third year of junior high school, Uncle Hyōei began studying for the university entrance exams, aiming to enter the Department of Sciences and Engineering at Waseda University. My brother was one of those entrusted with this secret; I saw this, and as his younger brother I felt proud. After Uncle Hyōei passed the entrance exams, his father refused to pay his school fees. If Uncle Hyōei had entered the Buddhist university that he was originally supposed to attend, there would have been no need for entrance and tuition fees. Uncle Hyōei's father probably felt that taking this stern position would cause his son to return to his original course. Our family was poorer than Uncle Hyōei's family, yet we decided to offer support. In April, on the day that all the villagers take an excursion to view the cherry blossoms, there was a sake party beneath a beautiful cherry tree at the dilapidated temple; suddenly Uncle Hyōei's father dashed off to our house, where he stood in front, yelling insults at my father. My father liked to drink a large cup of sake before bed, but he never went to the afternoon cherry-blossom parties. When he appeared in the doorway with a sour look on his face, the treasurer's attitude changed completely.

He began to thank my father repeatedly while reaching out to squeeze his hands. "What kind of parent would put a child in such a predicament?" he exclaimed in a loud voice. During the summer vacation, Uncle Hyōei returned home with a Waseda University cap on his large head. He gave me a children's comic book called "Fuku-chan," about a child who wore an oversized cap.

About that time, my mother, while trying to control herself, had to express her opinion to my father. (I didn't hear about this until long after my father's death.) If he were to assist Uncle Hyōei against the treasurer's wishes, problems would be likely to arise; it is children's immediate families who are most concerned about their lives, and so we surely shouldn't intervene. My father did not oppose mother's reasoning, but responded in this way: "Uncle Hyōei is a great man." (My father, like all the relatives, referred to him as "Uncle," which caused some confusion. Probably even Lévi-Strauss's theory can't explain how a person can be an uncle to both my father and myself.) "He plans to study the natural sciences and combine this with the study of Buddhism," my father continued. "Uncle Hyōei says that he has already studied as much Buddhism as they teach at the university. It seems that Buddhism and the study of the natural sciences were originally closely related. Because I am not as learned as Uncle Hyōei, I am not in a position to oppose him."

As he told my mother, she also did not possess the scholarship to oppose Uncle Hyōei's intention to study the natural sciences and Buddhism together. But my mother was the sort of person who raised her children by any means possible; she knew how to live and had common sense. She harbored misgivings about Uncle Hyōei's future, and her common sense was shared by most people in the valley. Uncle Hyōei soon began to confirm their fears. Little by little he began to decline, and there were probably many who watched this development intently.

Uncle Hyōei returned to the valley in the summer of his second year at the university, and when fall came around he took no steps to return to Tokyo. He devoted himself to self-education. Again he restricted his reading to the domain of Buddhism; he also read the Bible. There was also talk that

he read the Koran, in order to understand it clearly, though I don't know what type of translation he could have obtained at that time.

Uncle Hyōei was exempt from military service—because of tuberculosis, everyone believed at first. But it soon became known that the reason was actually a mental disorder. It may have been in reaction to this rumor that Uncle Hyōei stopped asking my brother over to talk, and consequently I could no longer listen in on their discussions. Uncle Hyōei became an entirely solitary person. He had a sheep, whose back he would bundle with books; instead of using the big concrete bridge over the ravine, he would lead the sheep over the temporary bridge that people working in the fields had built by piling up rocks and placing planks over them. Then he would turn the sheep loose on the other bank, which was overgrown with grass, and read. Only when it had become completely dark would he return home, and then he would cross the larger bridge.

There were two kinds of rumor circulating among the children regarding Uncle Hyōei's behavior. One of these was not particularly harmful, but if the other were to reach the ears of an adult woman or her daughters, it might have serious consequences. The first rumor was that Uncle Hyōei walked around pulling a red string that was invisible to the normal human eye. Someone claimed to have heard the name of this string in Hindi. In order not to get the red string tangled up, Uncle Hyōei would pull it all in before he went to bed, and he avoided passing the same place twice in a day. This explained why he led his sheep across the wooden bridge in the early morning. This was the nicer of the two stories. The other rumor was that Uncle Hyōei stayed at the grassy area until dark because he would fornicate while standing up with the female sheep, which had already borne many lambs. That was why Uncle Hyōei gave off an extremely strong odor that was worse than the smell of anyone else who raised sheep.

I did not believe this story. An upper-grade student, with a big lunch box that would have been adequate for a mountain laborer, came from the neighboring village expressly to convince me: "A human's cunt and a sheep's are very similar. In the case of humans, we are accustomed to seeing it from the front; in the

case of sheep, they are accustomed to looking at it from behind. That is the only difference.''

I was not at all accustomed to looking at a woman's reproductive organs from the front. And if a ewe's genitals, which I glimpsed now and then from behind, were the same as a woman's, a great mystery of life would have been revealed by trivial chance. According to this story, Uncle Hyōei would drop his old trousers to his heels and hold on tight to the terrified ewe—an image that seemed so sad it made me want to cry. At that time I thought well of Uncle Hyōei; maybe it was because he somehow understood this that he gave me those valuable books when my father died.

Soon after the war was lost, something happened to Uncle Hyōei, a temporary change that transformed him. My older brother had once been his conversational partner, while I listened in. But now my brother had returned from military training camp and was contemptuous toward Uncle Hyōei. He had become a soldier, he said, while Uncle Hyōei was playing around with his sheep in the grassy thicket at the riverbank. So Uncle Hyōei made me his pupil. The big change was that he began working as a substitute teacher of English at the new-system junior high school in the valley. Uncle Hyōei was assigned to the grade I was in, and in his mind I was the only student. Another substitute teacher, who had emigrated to the valley from the city, used an American conversation textbook. Choruses of "Hello, nice to see you!" could be heard as far as the playground. But Uncle Hyōei centered his teaching on the basics of pronunciation. "As far as teaching English is concerned, I don't know about the other children, but for the future study of foreign languages, it is important for you, K-chan, to know the basics." He mimeographed the pages on pronunciation from the textbook he had used as a student at the old-system junior high school, and used those to teach the class. For a full year we memorized the phonetic symbols and devoted ourselves to practicing pronunciation. Although this was a natural method, the classes were so dull that they became painful. Since even I— Uncle Hyōei's chosen student—felt this way, there is no need to say how the others felt. A year went by, and it was clear why Uncle Hyōei was not reappointed to his position. As if nothing

had changed after the chaotic end of the war, he once again began living in seclusion with his old, feeble sheep, which could no longer provide milk.

Because I was a favorite of Uncle Hyōei's, I felt ashamed at not having opposed his expulsion. Very early in the morning, while I was still in bed, I would hear Uncle Hyōei crossing the wooden bridge and scolding the sheep he had loved for many years. (The entrance to the bridge was built over a wide shoal right behind our house.) When I heard this, I would hold my breath and listen, feeling guilty. "Hey! You're a complete fool! Can't you understand when I tell you this?" (I would hear the sheep's feet stamping in fright on the planks, hear its pathetic cry.) "Hey, you, hey! That's the morning sun shining on the water! It isn't a knife to cut your throat with! Hey, you, hey! No matter how time passes, you're still a fool, aren't you? Around here everybody's a fool!"

Shortly afterward I left the valley to attend the new-system high school in the neighboring village. Although I planned to return to the village soon, it has been more than thirty years already since I've been back to the valley except for school holidays. According to Eliade, the village that a person leaves in childhood or adolescence assumes a mythical form. Even now, while staying at the Berkeley Faculty Club, I have dreams of returning to the village with my Tokyo-born children. Uncle Hyōei's class has left one mark: when I talk to someone in English, my tics of pronunciation create confusion— in other words, I have not been able to correct the distorted pronunciation taught by Uncle Hyōei. For example, I couldn't really learn to pronounce the uncommon, narrow sound of the first syllable of "Berkeley" without converting it to one of the basic phonetic sounds.

What was my relationship with Uncle Hyōei later, in the real world? Except for that first year after Japan's defeat in the war, Uncle Hyōei lived in seclusion, beginning midway through the war on. I was closer to Uncle Hyōei during his last years, even if only geographically, than were any of his immediate family. We even spoke several times. Suddenly, nearly twenty-five years after the war, Uncle Hyōei came to the capital. When he reached

Tokyo, he led a vagabond life, first at Takadanobaba Station, near Waseda, where he had attended the university, and later on the grounds of the Shinjuku train and subway station.

A newspaper article appeared; perhaps some of you may remember it. "Pulled by five sheep, an old Buddhist philosopher heads toward Tokyo from the depths of the Shikoku forests." That was indeed what Uncle Hyōei did. He had taken five descendants of that ewe who had mistaken the reflection of the morning sun for the glistening of the slaughterhouse knife and trained them for a long time—angrily scolding them as he encouraged them to pull the cart—just as he had studied for the Department of Sciences and Engineering entrance exams.

Uncle Hyōei's family was indifferent to his journey. As Uncle Hyōei was preparing to leave the valley, his nephew (now the head of the family) and the others had predicted that the sheep would probably refuse to go on after leaving the valley, since they had resided in the forest for generation after generation. Uncle Hyōei was setting out for Tokyo, but he probably wouldn't get any farther than the ferryboat port. Even if he got that far, the ferryboat would probably not allow on board a cart pulled by five sheep and packed with cooking utensils, bedding, and books. In short, no one could take seriously the extremely capricious action of this elderly recluse. On the morning he set off on his long journey, he had walked down the stone road from the Mountain Temple, where he had been living. As he passed the kitchen of the main house, his nephew's wife turned and looked over her shoulder for just an instant while preparing breakfast. In an indifferent voice, she called out, "You're leaving? You're really leaving?" The sky surrounding the forest was completely clear, and a cool wind was passing over the village.

Shinjuku Station is where he was living when I went to visit him. He had drunk a little beer or sake and seemed somewhat uninhibited; when I talked with him, he responded. It was an unusual opportunity for me to listen to him; usually he said little. He said that his nephew's wife had been wearing her high-school-aged daughter's T-shirt. The way she turned her neck to look over her shoulder was nice and sexy, said Uncle Hyōei, as if he had reverted to his Waseda days. "It was a Felix the Cat shirt," he added. By the time he began his journey, Uncle Hyōei

had overcome his fastidious abhorrence of women, and he was in a frame of mind in which he could generously accept even something that was slightly sexy. As I mentioned earlier, among the books I have with me is the Iwanami Library edition of *The Buddha's Last Journey (Maha Pari Nirvana Sutra)*. As the Buddha traveled for the last time on earth, he met a prostitute, Ann Pavari, who served him "delicious food to chew and drink." The Buddha gladly accepted her kindness. Uncle Hyōei's nephew's wife did not offer even a bowl of miso soup—she only turned around, revealing her neck and shoulders and the shirt she was wearing with Felix the Cat—but . . .

Even people who knew of Uncle Hyōei's long reclusive life and who thought that such a whimsical person was not the type to be taken seriously began to think that he might achieve some success, perhaps in preaching to the public. It was the newspaper article I mentioned earlier that was responsible for this change. The regional metropolitan newspaper, the only one in the prefecture, had ignored him when he passed through. But an article with a postcard-sized photo of Uncle Hyōei appeared on the national page of a central paper. According to our relatives, the bureau reporter, who was an alumnus of Waseda University, seemed to be in an antiestablishment mood of the time. When I read the paper that morning, I saw the whitish beard and the closed-collar jacket of Uncle Hyōei, who looked exactly like Ho Chi Minh with his thin yet big-boned body and his ears that stuck out on either side of his childlike face. Having felt a blood kinship in the picture, I was convinced that I would someday look like this old man. Furthermore, at Uncle Hyōei's knees were the triumphant faces of the sheep. "Surely they cannot be Uncle Hyōei's children?" I couldn't resist asking this indecent question.

Even the bureau reporter, who was friendly to Uncle Hyōei, said that he spoke very little. The article mentioned that he was traveling with his sheep to Tokyo with the intention of elucidating the teachings of the Buddha to the people, especially to confused youth; otherwise it did not give much specific information. Uncle Hyōei "lived on ascetic meals of sheep's milk and bread crusts. When I invited him for a meal and a cup of sake at a restaurant, he just sat without speaking, but he

good-heartedly accepted my invitation." So the article ended. In the *Maha Pari Nirvana Sutra* there is a strikingly similar phrase: "The Buddha maintained his silence and indicated his assent." The newspaper that printed the article takes pride in having the largest circulation of any paper; because of its influence, Uncle Hyōei had no trouble boarding the ferryboat. From Takamatsu, he safely crossed over to Uno. He was now on the mainland. No longer separated from Tokyo, Uncle Hyōei and his sheep could reach the city on foot merely by advancing in the right direction.

During the harsh winter months—it was a year of heavy snowfall in western Japan—Uncle Hyōei and his five sheep took shelter at the Akashi Temple; this prolonged the journey considerably. In mid-April, I received a phone call from the village. I was told that Uncle Hyōei had reached Tokyo, had already left Takadanobaba Station, and had begun to live the life of a vagrant at Shinjuku Station. As soon as I laid eyes on him at the east entrance of the station, I knew this was the life he had adopted. It had been a long time since I had learned English pronunciation from him at the new-system junior high school. Uncle Hyōei looked up at me—a man now, no longer a youth—with suspicion, but also with an expression that revealed an inner poise. He sat like an Indian yogi, his lap covered with old quilts and rags, with his back against a square pillar. The place was well chosen to avoid the wind. Uncle Hyōei's whole face seemed to have grown darker: his cheeks, his chin, even his gray beard. Frankly, he was black with dirt and filth, but his odor was cloaked by a quaint, musty smell, strong but not unpleasant, as if he had been burning incense. His glittering eyes seemed to reveal a certain indomitable spirit. As he turned those deep eyes on me, I gradually began to recognize in him the Uncle Hyōei I had known.

I knelt at his side and continued to talk to him. It could scarcely be called a conversation; Uncle Hyōei "maintained his silence and indicated his refusal." He did finally tell me that all of his sheep had been killed by a pack of stray dogs on a hillside at the Yokohama Foreigners' Cemetery. "There aren't even any mountain dogs in the depths of the forest!" he lamented angrily. He was referring to the strays in the valley, whose numbers had increased rapidly after the war when food shortages made it

impossible for families to keep their dogs. The children in the valley called these strays "mountain dogs" and were terrified of them. I remembered this with a deep nostalgia. In addition, I felt that Uncle Hyōei and I had established a connection through our shared experiences in the village in the valley.

This was our first meeting. I continued to pay calls of respect to Uncle Hyōei at Shinjuku Station, sometimes accompanied by my wife. Uncle Hyōei's nephew and my mother asked me to try to persuade Uncle Hyōei to return home. Uncle Hyōei's nephew himself came to Tokyo to urge him to return, but Uncle Hyōei "remained silent, indicating refusal." His behavior grew increasingly obstinate; I suspected that he was suffering from a psychological disorder.

I could get only a small number of words out of Uncle Hyōei during the hundred days that he lived at Shinjuku Station. He had planted himself on the ground right in the stream of commuter traffic, as if it had been his home for many years. It was extraordinarily painful to squat down while exchanging words with Uncle Hyōei. (If you try squatting, you'll see why.) When passers-by bumped into my back, they would glare much more at me than at the vagrant beside me, with eyes that frowned upon any antisocial existence. After a month of living at Shinjuku Station, Uncle Hyōei became indistinguishable from any other vagrant who publicly urinated and got drunk—in fact, he finally became worse than the others. And yet, when I would urge him to return to the village, Uncle Hyōei always stood firm and "remained silent, indicating refusal."

At this time I was feeling aloof to Uncle Hyōei. My decision to leave him among the vagrants rather than pursue a more constructive plan had much to do, I think, with the fact that I was now over thirty. It was a period when I began to think that each person has to find his own way of living; even if what he does deviates from common sense, there are things that one cannot interfere with from outside. This holds true even if the person is elderly. Sometimes, when I passed through the eastern subway entrance of Shinjuku Station, I happened to see Uncle Hyōei leaning against a square pillar, trying to sleep or to cover himself with rags. He was practicing what he had taught us. "At any rate, Uncle Hyōei, 'Like a rhinoceros's horn, you walk alone,'" I'd

mutter. (That was a Buddhist expression the young Uncle Hyōei had taught my older brother.) I even harbored encouraging thoughts about the way he was living. If my relatives wanted to call me irresponsible in my conduct toward him—which, in fact, they did—well, so be it.

Unlike me, my wife often went to give him a little money or to replace his underwear and medicine. She later took over the principal responsibility of passing along information about Uncle Hyōei to the village in the valley. The family leaned toward having Uncle Hyōei taken away by the police so that he might be forced into a hospital or some sort of institution. According to my wife, only my mother thought that we should let him be as he wanted to be for a while.

Once when my wife went to call on Uncle Hyōei, she couldn't find him in his usual place. My wife has a unique way of dealing with circumstances: instead of inquiring with the police or the station authorities, she went around asking the vagrants, and eventually found Uncle Hyōei beside the public rest room, far from the station grounds. Uncle Hyōei told her about the enthusiastic student demonstrations that were frequently taking place at the station at that time. These demonstrations were causing some problems: "Last night, 'There was not even enough space to insert the tip of a rabbit's hair,'" explained Uncle Hyōei, once again using an expression from Buddhist scriptures. However, his migration had nothing to do with the student demonstrations; rather, he was suffering from diarrhea. On that day he was particularly pleased to accept the underwear. Uncle Hyoei, who seemed to have become talkative, especially with women, said that on the Buddha's last journey, which led to his death, he had contracted a severe case of diarrhea after eating a meal of mushrooms offered by the blacksmith Gunda. So Uncle Hyōei could accept his diarrhea as something to be expected. But then he suddenly became angry. "Don't people in Tokyo know what to throw away and what not to throw away? They shouldn't be throwing out things in clean paper bags that people will pick up and eat and get a stomach ache from! Dogs can tell by smell what is safe to eat and what isn't. But humans have lost this sense!" In recalling this incident, my wife said to me, "You should grow into an old man who can get magnificently angry

like that." In saying this, she was displaying a strange logic, as if she were nostalgic about something that lay ahead in the future.

When Uncle Hyōei first undertook his journey to the capital, he had expected to have students and other young people as his audience; however, they nonchalantly betrayed his unrealistic hopes. That Saturday, the students gathering on the station grounds ran into trouble with the station authorities. The newspaper reported that the police had been called in, and also that a vagrant who lived in the station had been injured in the clash. I had a strong suspicion as to who this vagrant might be, and on Sunday I went down to the station. I searched thoroughly and discovered Uncle Hyōei by the underground food stands of the department store nearby. He was lying on some newspapers on the landing of a short staircase, curled up to protect the injured right side of his belly and using his elbow as a pillow. He seemed to have shrunk a size and to be avoiding pedestrians as he lay close to the wall. He was intently watching a piece of dust that was being swirled around by the wind along the base of the wall, and did not respond to my call.

That evening my wife went to the station with a boxed meal, some tea, and an aluminum can of sake. Uncle Hyōei had already returned to his former spot and was sitting upright against his pillar. In front of my wife, he drank the can of sake in one swallow. When she asked if he would like her to go and buy another, he declined. He said that the students had no knowledge of Buddhism. They were headstrong and unwilling to listen to other people; the windows of the five senses, which should be open to the wisdom of truth, were closed. The night before, Uncle Hyōei had joined one of the many small groups of youths in the demonstration. When he challenged the group, they treated him like a nuisance and pushed him aside so roughly that he fell. The pain in the side of his abdomen seemed to be persisting. My wife urged him to see a doctor, but he said quietly that if he did he would be forced into an institution or sent back to the country. He said that he might have broken a rib. "However, when people are my age, their bones, and their muscles, too, are already wearing out, so even if I am left alone in this condition, I will be able to live through my allotted portion of life as well as I can, won't I!"

For the first time, he even began to talk about my work. Uncle Hyōei called me "K-chan" as he had when I was a new-system junior high school student. "Broken bones, broken muscles, why think so much about fixing them? It's all the same: everything will pass away. Tell K-chan not to think too much about useless things. Just keep on with his ascetic training— that's my advice!" Here he was quoting a passage from the *Maha Pari Nirvana Sutra.* Uncle Hyōei, at any rate, considered my writing novels to be one form of ascetic training.

About ten days after this incident, I was leaving Shinjuku Station by the east exit on my way to speak at a university assembly. Uncle Hyōei would have thought it a sheer waste of time, since our students were no longer eager to learn. It was late in the afternoon on a day that felt more like the beginning of winter than the end of autumn; where the light from outside and the illumination of the station subtly merged, I saw Uncle Hyōei sitting in the rusty golden light.

Uncle Hyōei was reverently holding something that looked like the ear of a cattail, which he ate slowly, savoring the taste ever so slowly with his mouth and tongue. I stopped about ten meters away, not wanting to interrupt what I saw. With his right arm Uncle Hyōei held a chopstick in front of his chest, keeping his elbow by his side, and slowly, as if in meditation, ate the fried sausage that was stuck onto it, savoring the chewing, the flavor, then swallowing. He protected his other side with his left arm; sitting in the familiar position of a yogi, with his long white beard covering his face and with the fried sausage held before him, it was as if he had been fossilized in his firm thoughts and vast loneliness. Only his mouth and Adam's apple were slowly, stiffly, reverently continuing to move.

I left for the meeting and gave my talk, but when I returned home I quickly acted on a plan I had been thinking about even during my lecture. I phoned my mother in the valley and told her that this seemed to be a good time to take Uncle Hyōei back to the Mountain Temple; if we worked on it now, he wouldn't resist and would peacefully come home. The next day, Uncle Hyōei's nephew and his wife flew to the capital. I don't know how to explain this, but my strong conviction was entirely correct: just as I had predicted to my mother, Uncle Hyōei did not object to

returning to the forest. He settled down, not in a corner of the reconstructed Mountain Temple but in a wing on the grounds of his nephew's house. A doctor in our family confirmed that Uncle Hyōei's ribs were broken and had penetrated the surrounding tissue. Even so, he did not enter the hospital. During the first severe cold snap of the winter, Uncle Hyōei caught pneumonia. I would like to write that he died without suffering much.

Well, now I am living at the faculty club on the grounds of an American university. Actually—I've been reluctant to write this until now—I am staying at the Women's Faculty Club. Occasionally, while eating frozen vegetables stir-fried with instant noodles, I savor the tiny pieces on my tongue, one by one, slowly, without hurrying. There are times when the gestures of this middle-aged body and soul still repeat those of Uncle Hyōei. Then I say, in a muffled voice, "Hey? Hey!"

—Translated by Mari Hoashi with Masao Miyoshi

Maple on the Hill

October again. Faint pheasant tail
Slips through and ruffles the maple tree.
 A few feathers
Leaf down to cuckold the grass.
Power lines shine, cars shine.
 Season of glass-glint and edge,

Abracadabra of sunlight,
 cut and spin.
The day saws itself in half.
Northwest wind has something up its sleeve.
At the horned heart of the labyrinth,
 the unsayable has its say.

———

Don't forget me little darling, when they've laid me down to die.
Just one little wish, darling, that I pray.
As you linger there in sadness you are thinking of the past,
Let your teardrops kiss the flowers on my grave.

———

The mirror of history swallows its images:
It never repeats itself
 in us, its distorted children.
Each life, as Plutarch tells us,
Contains many lives,
 some recognizable, some not.

History's just another story.
In the City of the Dead, no one

 stands up and says, *Here I am, I'm your boy.*
Discontinuous, discrete,
The hunter, history's dog, will sniff us,

 sure as hell . . .

PETER NAGY

Time
Lines

Time Lines

p. 116 *Léger* (Cancer Logo series), 1985

p. 117 *To Die Alive,* 1990 (detail, pp. 118–19)

p. 120 *America Invented Everything* (Cancer Logo series), 1985

p. 121 *Urbanism and the Call to Prayer,* 1990 (detail, pp. 122–23)

p. 124 *Parasitical Clown Dough* (Cancer Logo series), 1986

p. 125 *You Adore Me,* 1990 (detail, pp. 126–27)

The Minor Manchu's Daughter

I forget my father every moment.
I tear his banner into bird-sized rags
and throw them to the wind.
I have a coin he once gave me.
I tried to bring myself to spend it
but a beggar danced in my gut. He nagged
and nagged. As if I were his friend
he spouted his sorry lines. He pleaded.
I forget my father every day.
In his grave. In his humble sandals
that shied away from mountains.
I set my heart on those mountains.
They are steep and rich and full
of change. I'll lose my mother along the way.

What Way is Left?

Social Change in the Postindustrial Age

Interview by John Keane

Keane: You've been arguing for ten years or more that full employment is a thing of the past, that it has become economically impossible as a result of a set of technical transformations that are also known as the "microelectronics revolution." In your view, Keynes is dead: full employment will not be reestablished by stimulating economic growth. Don't recent developments in both the United States and Europe show this argument to be ill founded?

Gorz: It all depends on what you mean by "full employment." In the past, the term referred to a situation in which everyone could find a full-time job, lasting all year, from the time they left school until they retired. We shall never see that again. In all the industrially developed countries, between 40 and 50 percent of the active population are in what is called "atypical" employment—precarious, part-time, temporary, or short-term jobs with periods of unemployment in between. This is as true in Western Europe as in the United States.

The "death of Keynes" was announced as long ago as the early '70s in a study by the German metalworkers' union in Frankfurt, which showed that robotization not only reduces the amount of labor required but also saves capital. In other words,

the more you invest in industry, the more jobs you eliminate, and that includes jobs in the engineering industries. The "productivity of capital" increases alongside the productivity of labor. *Fortune* magazine has published several studies of individual enterprises illustrating this fact, most notably one dated May 25, 1987, on the Japanese firm Fanuc, where the manufacture of robots has itself been robotized. In one of its entirely automated plants, "70 workers and 130 robots produce 18,000 motors a month. The plant cost $32 million, which is around a tenth of what a conventional factory would have cost, and it requires only one-tenth as many workers."

Keane: Many economists would argue that you exaggerate the importance of productivity gains. They say these are happening much more slowly overall than in the '60s, and the problem is not that they are too rapid but that they are insufficient.

Gorz: Statistically, that's right. But you have to see why. You have, roughly speaking, two sectors in modern economies. In the first of these, the microelectronics revolution is bringing very rapid productivity gains. These are distinctly more rapid than in the past, on the order of 10 to 12 percent per year in the automotive industry, for example. In the second sector, which covers services that cannot be industrialized (personal services, teaching, advertising, decorating, etc.), productivity is progressing slowly or not at all. Now, as a direct result of increasing productivity, the number of workers in the first sector is constantly falling, whereas the number in the second sector is rising, because that is the only place where extra jobs can be created, one way or another.

Twenty years ago, workers in industry represented something like 40 percent of the work force in West Germany, Italy, and Great Britain. When the productivity of labor increased by 7 percent in industry and by 2 percent in other activities, it grew by 4 percent within the economy as a whole. Currently, workers in industry represent barely 30 percent of the working population. Now, even if their productivity increased by nearly 10 percent, the 4 percent rise in overall annual productivity would be reached only if the productivity of services also rose,

for its part, by 1.5 to 2 percent. But such a rise is quite out of the question, because the main function of the very high—and constantly growing—proportion of services is to create jobs for people who would otherwise be unemployed, even if the jobs created are totally irrational from the economic point of view. This is what I have called the "tertiary anti-economy," since its objective is to ensure that a maximum amount of paid labor is consumed, while the modern economy has the opposite goal, seeking to reduce the quantity of labor required per unit of production.

If, for example, you take the jobs created in the last ten years or so in the United States, you will find that most of those jobs have the following function: the two hours you used to spend mowing your lawn, walking your dog, going to fetch your paper, doing your housework, or looking after your children are transferred to a service-provider who does those tasks in your stead, for payment. That person does nothing that you couldn't do yourself. He or she merely frees up two hours of your time by enabling you to buy two hours of his or her time. This type of transfer is the essential characteristic of servants' work, and even the founding fathers of political economy insisted that work done by servants is economically unproductive. Moreover, this type of employment only develops in conditions of extreme inequality. The new servants offer their services to private individuals because they can't find jobs within the social process of production, and it's only in the interest of private individuals to buy other people's time if two hours of their own working time bring in distinctly more than they pay for two hours of the servants' time. The "service society," based on the development of personal services, is necessarily a "dual society."

Keane: Yet neoliberals suggest that the technological revolution will have universally beneficial effects if only it is allowed to proceed unhindered. They defend policies designed to loosen market rigidities and to abolish state regulations on employees and investors. "Be flexible or perish" is the new motto, and we're now seeing an unprecedented cult of private enterprise bravely battling for its market share.

Gorz: But the microelectronics revolution wasn't launched by private enterprise. Its origins lie in the billions of dollars of public money invested by the American government in its military and space program. In Japan, where it developed most quickly, that technological revolution was promoted voluntarily by the Ministry of International Trade and Industry, working together with industry and the big banks. Microprocessors, biotechnologies, and nuclear and photovoltaic energy were all based initially on research and development financed by the state. In Europe, even industrial giants like Philips and Siemens agreed to take on the joint development of a 4-megabyte "chip" only on condition that they receive public funding for it.

Neoliberals always argue as if capital were invested spontaneously where unsatisfied needs are at their greatest. This has never been the case. Capital is invested where it can be sure of the highest returns. Producing to meet the most pressing needs of the needier sections of the population is never the best way to make the most money. The way to do that is to produce goods or services likely to appeal to the most prosperous strata. That is why the liberalization of the economy always begins by impoverishing the poor and enriching the rich. This was obvious in the last century and it is again today, not only in Bush's America or Thatcher's Britain, but also throughout the rest of Europe. If you examine the sectors in which exacerbated competition between enterprises is speeding up technical innovation, improving product quality, and increasing productivity, you mainly find products aimed at the most prosperous segment of the population, while the standard of living of the people at the bottom of the wage ladder is continually deteriorating, as are their living conditions.

The free play of market mechanisms leads, then, to social decline, and contrary to what many neoliberals argue, that social decline is not accompanied by economic boom. In fact, the opposite is true. The three European countries that have the most efficient economies and the highest technical standards—Sweden, Switzerland, and West Germany—are precisely the ones where strong trade-union power makes the labor market more rigid, hinders price competition, and maintains higher

wages and better working conditions than elsewhere. Taking everything into account, wage costs are 30 percent higher there than in France and 50 percent higher than in Britain. And that is why the productivity of labor and the rate of innovation are highest there. It is much more difficult in these countries—particularly in Sweden—to hire and fire temporary workers, so Swedish companies are forced to make unparalleled efforts to train their work forces and reorient their production. The result is that the Swedish economy is probably the most flexible and efficient in the world. Where it is relatively easy to take on and lay off temporary workers and to employ a very low-cost work force, as in Britain or France, technical innovation is less rapid and product quality lower.

Keane: In all the countries of Europe, from the Atlantic to the Urals, virtually everyone today is in favor of the unhindered play of market mechanisms. Yet in your writings you argue for an increasing restriction of the sphere of commodity exchange. You are one of the few still to claim a central role for planning and for public control of macroeconomic decisions. But aren't market mechanisms, contrary to what Marx thought, something more than—and other than—characteristics of "bourgeois" society? Aren't they necessary to some extent, if only to prevent shortages and bottlenecks? And doesn't the idea of abolishing commodity relations to make room for the self-management of production and exchange bear the imprint of last century's egalitarian utopias, which simply cannot be translated into reality?

Gorz: You are quite right that there can be no complex society without commodity relations or markets. The total abolition of market relations would presuppose the abolition of the social division and specialization of labor and thus the return to autarkic communities or a society of kibbutzim. Ursula Le Guin conjured up a planetary kibbutz of this kind in her novel *The Dispossessed*, which is the most striking description I know of the seductions—and snares—of a self-managed communist or, in other words, anarchist society.

But we have to be clear first of all about what the terms "commodity relations," "free competition," and "market economy" mean. "Commodity relations" means exchanges based on buying and selling in which what is being bought or sold takes the commodity form. You sell to me, I pay you, we are quits, and our relationship can end there. I have shown elsewhere that this buying and selling relationship is only rational and functional when the output of the object or service being sold is measurable and where it therefore lends itself to quantitative evaluation. If it includes personal involvement, a "gift of oneself," it is no longer possible to be quits by paying for it, whatever the price paid. It impoverishes and depersonalizes the fabric of emotional life and human relationships if commodity relations and monetarization are extended to the furnishing of nonquantifiable goods and services, which only achieve their purpose if money is not their goal. The more we extend the sphere of activities about which we can say "This is not for sale" or "I can't put a price on this," the richer are our individual and social lives.

Yet the existence of commodity relations does not necessarily imply the existence of a real market. Goods can be bought and sold at prices set by convention, in conformity with centuries-old tradition, or at prices fixed by the state. In this latter case, competing sellers do not directly confront buyers seeking to buy at the best price. The sellers are not therefore forced by competition to seek maximum productivity of the factors of production. This has advantages as well as disadvantages, as Max Weber and Karl Polanyi—not to mention Plato and the Christian theologians—have shown.

Lastly, there may be commodity relations and competition on markets without there being a true market economy. And indeed you made the distinction yourself in speaking of "market mechanisms" without using the term "market economy." The fact is that the market economy is an economy in which prices are established freely, in every sector, at a level where supply and demand reach equilibrium, without intervention or manipulation or hindrance of any kind. Do you know a single country whose economy is regulated in that way?

Keane: The answer is certainly no, except for the land of pure capitalism that exists in the heads of certain neoliberals.

Gorz: If the price of agricultural produce or the level of wages were determined by the laws of supply and demand, most of us would long ago have died of starvation. In all the industrial nations, the relative prices of goods and services are regulated by the state; if they weren't, society wouldn't be viable. Everything that's vital is subsidized: agricultural production, housing, health, transport, education, libraries, research, museums, theaters, etc. And the rest is taxed to varying degrees by a system of VAT or specific taxes—on petroleum products, alcohol, tobacco and matches, etc. The more extensive the sphere of commodity relations, the more the state has to intervene in the market mechanisms to correct and regulate their functioning. The fact is that the market is, by definition, the outcome of the activities of individuals each pursuing his or her own immediate interests. Thus a higher authority, the state, is required to take responsibility for defending the general interest, including the existence of a market system.

Keane: This brings us to the fundamental question: To what extent must market mechanisms be allowed free play?

Gorz: This is the question that has been at the heart of political conflict for two hundred years. Commodity relations, by which I mean the freedom of each individual to pursue his or her own immediate interests, tend to destroy both civil society and the general conditions that make them possible. The nature and extent of the advantages that an individual has the right to procure for him- or herself must therefore be restricted by law. The history of capitalism is the history of a continual extension of these legal restrictions: the abolition of slavery; antimonopoly and antitrust legislation; the prohibition of the sale of children and women; the prohibition of child labor; Sunday as a rest day; the ten-hour and then the eight-hour work day; the legal minimum wage; legal standards for quality, safety, hygiene, and pollution; universal health insurance; old age pensions; and so on.

The basic problem is that this way of limiting and correcting

market mechanisms does not prevent the destruction of civil society. The welfare state can, to a certain extent, limit the scope of that destruction, but overall it functions as a substitute for a civil society that is in the process of withering away. In some respects, it even hastens the process of decay. I'm entirely in agreement with the way you treat this question in *Democracy and Civil Society:* there can't be socialism without democracy and there can't be democracy without a much more substantial civil society comprising a set of self-organized public activities recognized and protected by the state. Socialism was born out of a conflict between civil society and the market. It took off as a movement by demanding that market forces be contained, subdued, and controlled by society, whereas capitalism presented the opposite demand. However, for society to control market forces and place economic rationality in the service of societal and cultural ends, it is necessary, first, that society have an autonomous existence, and second, that the market exist or has existed and that economic agents have been coerced by it into economically rational behavior, i.e., the pursuit of maximum efficiency in putting the factors of production to work.

For us, in the capitalist countries, the first point is the most important. It implies that a socialist politics cannot be content merely to correct and regulate the operation of the market through state controls and services financed by the state. It must promote the development of a sphere of lived sociality (what the Germans call *soziale Lebenswelt*) made up of forms of self-organized, voluntary cooperation and of noncommodity, nonmonetary exchange. It must promote the social control of markets by citizens working together, and not merely by the public authorities. The question of what must be produced and how, the question of social priorities, of models of consumption, of styles of life—all this is currently decided by technocrats, businessmen, and bankers. Socialism would have to mean the democratization of these decisions, their public discussion at the level of associations, trade unions, movements, public hearings, and elected assemblies, and it would also have to mean taking into account criteria with which technocrats and company directors do not normally concern themselves.

Keane: When you call for social forms of control of markets, that implies you've given up the idea of a planned public sector, which you advocated in the past, at least for the production of necessities.

Gorz: In the 1960s, planning was all the fashion. Today all forms of planning and public ownership are condemned, both in the East and in the West. Currently the "market" is in vogue and is supposed to provide the necessary regulation and adjustments in an ideal way. This doesn't hold water. A complex economy cannot do without certain forms of planning. And planning is not incompatible either with the existence of markets or with the most varied forms of ownership, whether these be public, private, cooperative, or municipal.

If you rely solely on private initiative, on the market, you get into blind alleys. In China, for example, thousands of entrepreneurs all over the place set about manufacturing refrigerators, which is relatively easy and very profitable in the short run, only to find that the steel industry didn't produce enough sheet metal, since you can't set up the plants for producing that overnight; it requires long-term investment and infrastructures that depend on public funding. No industry, no large- or medium-scale enterprise, can dispense with planning its amortization, its investments, its labor needs, its purchases of raw materials and components several years ahead, and coordinating its plans with industries further up the line and with the public authorities. And the same obviously goes for public services such as education, transport, insurance, roads, and water distribution. Or for agricultural production, in which the free operation of the market and individual initiative lead, as in the four-year pig cycle, to overproduction with a collapse of prices, followed by shortages and skyrocketing prices, and so on. These cyclical fluctuations, which bankrupt an increasing proportion of producers, can be avoided only if the producers organize into associations and set targets that are not to be exceeded for each type of produce. This is called the organization of markets and is, in fact, an example of corporatist self-organization.

I cannot see why a complex society should not seek to

coordinate all these sectoral plans, both private and public, and to define medium- and long-term priorities, orientations, and goals for the whole of the economy. What I am talking about, in short, is a "framework plan." In reality, the question is not whether there should be planning or not, but who plans and in whose interest they plan.

The economic failure of the countries of Central and Eastern Europe was due not to the principle of planning but to the conditions and the methods employed. These prevented enterprises not only from competing but from even knowing what their costs were, and were thus an obstacle to the adoption of economically rational behavior. Moreover, instead of reining in the operation of the economy to make it serve society, they forced society to serve the creation of an economic apparatus. The result was a nonsociety and a noneconomy—the very opposite of socialism.

Yet the point is that it is quite possible to plan and socially control the adjustment of supply and demand without suppressing either competition between enterprises or the knowledge of costs.

Keane: The emphasis you place on the reduction of working hours may seem surprising when we look more closely at the transformations that technological changes have brought about in working conditions and labor relations. Weren't the allergic reaction to work and the refusal of work, which were very widespread in the early '70s, due to the repetitive character of jobs in the Taylorized factory or office? Isn't capitalist production increasingly using what Sabel and Piore call "flexible specialization" in highly computerized production units in which the old semiskilled workers have given way to teams of multiskilled operators who are highly trained, enjoy a great degree of autonomy, and are more like craftworkers than old-style semiskilled workers? Don't you underestimate the reskilling of workers, the rebirth of genuine craftwork as a result of computerization?

Gorz: There have always been two tendencies within the labor movement: the glorification of work and the aspiration to work

less. Those who glorified work were, for the most part, skilled workers who wielded great technical power within the factories. It seemed to them that it ought to be possible to transform that power into political power: they thought the workers should collectively appropriate the means of production, become the dominant class, and make the economy function for the benefit of all. The glorification of labor was therefore also a way of highlighting the strength of the working class. The more the workers identified with their role in production, the more they cast doubt on the solidity and legitimacy of the bourgeoisie's power. Their work was the source of all wealth; the economy was based on industries and crafts with workers as numerous as soldiers in a great army: miners, steelworkers, boilermakers, navvies, etc.

But all that has completely changed. Identification with work and the glorification of work can no longer have the sense of an identification with the working class and a glorification of its might. This is a fact that certain sociologists—particularly sociologists of industrial labor relations—will not see. Whether consciously or not, they want to preserve within their analyses the idea of a working class that derives from its technical power an aspiration to exercise political power and take control of the means of production.

We must first of all situate the new multiskilled professional workers, who are autonomous in their work, in their context: labor is no longer the main productive force, and the length of working time is no longer the measure of wealth. Enterprises are replacing human work by computer-integrated automatic systems, which produce more, better, and more flexibly with a smaller and smaller fraction of the work force previously required. Semiskilled workers and laborers are increasingly being eliminated from industry, but so are the traditional craftworkers in the metalworking industries, such as toolmakers, millers, and fitters. Machine tools controlled by microprocessors and flexible manufacturing systems no longer require those skills. Industry needs people who are capable of independent teamwork and of coordinating their initiatives and skills without having anyone to supervise them or give them orders. They have to take responsibility for a complex system of machines and

robots that, above all, require maintenance and immediate repair whenever there is the slightest breakdown. These new skilled workers have to be committed to their work. They have to be able to adapt to rapidly changing techniques and to acquire new skills, both manual and intellectual. For doing so, the enterprise offers them a privileged status and salary.

Keane: This trend is sometimes seen as a sign of the renewal of working-class attempts to achieve liberation or at least achieve control over production.

Gorz: That is laughable because the basic question is this: What fraction of the working class acquires these skills and this status? Today, less than 10 percent. Tomorrow that stratum of "modern expert workers," as Kern and Schumann call them, will come to represent 25 percent of the workers in industry, and perhaps even 40 percent in the metalworking industries, we are told. That's fine, but what will become of the other 75 or 60 percent? What will they end up as? We know the answer already: they will become "peripheral workers," condemned, as in years gone by, to perform the thankless unskilled tasks, with no possibility of career advancement. For the most part, they will become temporary workers, with a precarious status, who can be taken on and laid off again according to the needs of the moment.

But there is more. Peripheral workers and privileged new skilled workers make up a work force that is constantly declining. In the long term, industry is tending to employ fewer and fewer people. The question, therefore, is not merely, What fraction of the working class do the new privileged skilled workers represent? but also, What fraction of the working population does the working class represent? What do the others do, those who have been eliminated—how nice it would be to say "liberated"—from industrial work? How do they live? How much do they earn?

If work and involvement in industry are to have some meaning, it is impossible not to ask these questions. And if you ask them, it is impossible to rest content with the improvement of the conditions of one group of workers in one sector of industry, unless you are willing to see the new work elite become a

corporatist, conservative stratum, caring only for the defense of its privileges. It is impossible to take the existence of this elite as a pretext for glorifying work—all work—since it is precisely the work of this stratum that explains why jobs—full-time, permanent jobs—are no longer available for the unemployed and for workers in precarious employment. To glorify the work of an industrial elite when there aren't enough jobs to go around is no longer to glorify the strength of the working class, but rather to induce that elite to see itself as distinct from the working class and to break its ties of solidarity with it. And in fact this is what employers' propaganda is doing.

Keane: Overall, you are saying that technical change is destroying the working class. It is the working class that is disintegrating, not capitalism. You don't, then, believe anymore in the possible unity of the working class and its central importance to any strategy for transforming society?

Gorz: That's not what I'm saying. The front of labor—of trade-union struggle—remains crucial, but there is no central front anymore. Society won't be changed without a trade-union movement worthy of the name "movement," but the creative impulses most often come from elsewhere. The central conflict is located at a level much deeper than labor disputes. The worker elite is indeed a participant in this central conflict. I am not by any means saying that it is a corporatist and conservative stratum. I am saying only that we push it in that direction when we constantly invoke the work ethic and the ideology of productivism in a way that redounds to its credit. This is what Mrs. Thatcher did for ten years, with telling results. The task of the trade-union movement and trade-union policy is to open up a different path and other horizons for that elite. Instead of simply telling it that it is doing exciting work that we can identify with, we also have to tell it, in my opinion, that its work leads to there being less and less work for the rest of us. And that you can't seriously do work that leads to the elimination of work and at the same time exalt work as the essential source of each person's identity. For the new industrial skilled workers, identifying with their occupation can't mean

identifying with their job within a flexible manufacturing system while remaining deaf and blind to everything else. Identifying with their occupation means understanding it as a social skill to be exercised in a responsible way. In other words, it means stepping back from the function they perform in production and asking themselves what social, economic, and cultural ends it serves. In particular, it means considering the redistribution of work and the reduction of working hours as essential questions of the highest priority. It is, therefore, viewing work in the proper perspective, not identifying with it, that can lay the ground for trade-union power and unity. This is a basic difference from the traditional views of the working class and trade unionism.

Keane: Ten years ago, you called those who didn't identify with their work the "nonclass of nonworkers." You accorded them a crucial role in challenging capitalism. You were severely criticized for that view. How, in fact, can that movement ever become a coordinated social movement capable of sustained action to transform society? Moreover, hasn't mounting unemployment caused the allergy to wage labor, the nonidentification with it, to disappear and be replaced by a frantic search for paid jobs of any kind?

Gorz: What I called the "nonclass of nonworkers" wasn't an identifiable and organizable stratum but the appearance of a thoroughgoing cultural change, which has continued to gain ground ever since: individuals no longer identify with their work, even when it is interesting and skilled, because it usually appears to them as a functional specialization in the service of a mega-machine on which they have no hold. They no longer identify with their place in the social process of production, nor do they derive from it the sense of belonging to a class. The social order has disintegrated; neither in their occupational role, nor in family structures, nor in the spatial structuring of their surroundings can individuals find what the sociologists used to call a determinate "identity," a reassuring social image of what they are. They are thrown back on themselves and have to search for and develop themselves in ways that are not given in advance.

Paid work is at best one dimension among others of that quest; it is seldom the most important.

These themes have been variously developed since then. The Italian metalworkers' union, Fiom-CGIL, concluded in a quite recent report that "we are engaged in a process of social change as a result of which work now occupies only a minor place in people's lives. More precisely, work—paid work—is losing its central position. It is only valued when it has the quality of autonomous creative activity. Otherwise it is regarded merely as a way of earning a living." In their most recent writings, Franz Steinkühler, the leader of the German metalworkers' union in Frankfurt, and Bruno Trentin, secretary-general of the CGIL, state in almost identical terms that trade-union policy must consist of creating the social conditions that enable all individuals to realize their potential and fulfill themselves in activities of their own choice, whether paid or unpaid, and to choose their way of life and their working hours—within the framework, of course, of negotiated agreements.

This distancing from work is in no way confined to unskilled employees. Even among the most highly skilled, the capacity for autonomy and initiative exceeds the degree of autonomy allowed or demanded by the functional specialization of work, however complex and responsible this work may be. Unlike the traditional labor movement, people are challenging the system not as agents of production but as people who cannot identify with their work and are not satisfied by it. As citizens, residents of a particular area, users of a public service, members of an association, or parents, they see their paid work in a wider context and conclude that their skills could be better employed, that industry could use technologies less polluting and less energy-consuming, that their quality of life could be improved if the requirements of economic rationality were subordinated to those of ecology, if production decisions were not made to get the best possible return on the largest possible amount of capital.

You have, then, a multidimensional social movement that can no longer be defined in terms of class antagonisms and in which people's aim is to reappropriate an environment that the mega-tools have alienated from them, to regain control of their lives by

reappropriating the skills that have been taken from them by the expertocracies on which big business and big government base their domination. This movement is essentially a struggle for collective and individual rights to self-determination, integrity, individual sovereignty. That struggle concerns all the different strata of wage-earners. It is fought in many different fields, and the company level is not always and not necessarily the most important of these. That's why the trade-union movement has a future only if it expands beyond the workplace and equips itself with what Bruno Trentin calls "structures of movement," public forums accessible to all, and opens itself up to debate, to common action, to alliance with other movements.

Keane: All in all, then, you are advocating political coalitions, new solidarities, and new alliances: between wage-earners in stable employment and the unemployed and precariously employed; between movements and parties. But do you believe that attempts to forge these solidarities and alliances can succeed?

Gorz: The question doesn't arise in precisely these terms. It isn't a matter of building coalitions or alliances between specific or sectoral interests—between elite workers and the unemployed and precarious workers, for example—but of winning new freedoms, new rights, which are by nature universal. People who set out to win or defend rights don't form either coalitions or alliances: they strive for what seems to them to be the common good, and that is what gives the movement its unity. This is the case with the women's movement, the antiracist movement, and the movement for a healthy environment. The battle for a reduction in working hours can be understood in this same way, as a struggle for a set of rights and freedoms, which may obviously assume highly differentiated forms, but whose contents are the same for everybody: the right to learn, to study at any age (not simply to "retrain"), to bring up one's children, to engage in political or public activities, to stay at home with a sick or dying relative or friend, etc. These rights to what Marx calls "the free development of individuality" presuppose having not only the available time but also the right to the

self-management of one's time within relatively flexible limits.

No insurmountable difficulties are therefore raised by the idea of bringing together all the different strata of wage-earners in solidarity, provided that the campaign for reducing working hours takes into account the diversity of situations involved. A reduction in weekly working hours isn't necessarily in everyone's interest. It may best suit those with stable employment, since their jobs require regular and continuous presence at the workplace. For a large number of skilled personnel, however, a linear reduction of the working day and the working week is not a possibility, particularly in the case of computer programmers, designers, technicians involved in setting up and testing new installations, etc. A reduction in annual working hours in the form of weeks or months of extra leave, together with entitlement to sabbatical years, will be more appropriate for people in these occupations, since their work requires imagination, ideas, and the refreshing of multidisciplinary knowledge, all of which are less easily acquired at the workplace than in discussion, reading, travel, stepping back from the tasks of the moment and varying one's activities and interests. The idea that the specialist can only keep abreast of things by total devotion to his or her specialty bears no relation to reality. It merely serves the interests of a system of domination that seeks to imprison people in their specialist fields in order to prevent them from questioning, as citizens, the ends that the decision-makers are making them serve.

Lastly, there is that 40 to 50 percent of the working population for whom the economy offers only casual, temporary, part-time employment: the unemployed and the precarious workers. The shrinking of the volume of work needed by the economy, which could be a source of freedom if it were distributed to all, is imposed as a deprivation on this fraction of the working population. These people, who can be hired and fired at will, are paid only for the work they do, not for their availability and capacity to work during the periods of forced unemployment. If we examine their situation closely, we see that they are victims of a discrimination whose rationale is essentially ideological. They are used as an example to show

that only time actually worked entitles a person to remuneration and, therefore, that working time must remain the measure of wealth and social usefulness. Now, these basic principles of capitalist ideology are, in fact, breached where the majority of workers in stable employment are concerned. Maintenance technicians, operators and controllers of automated plants, medical personnel, and workers in emergency services are paid for their availability and their capacity to intervene, not for work actually done. The ideology of maximum efficiency and of basing wages on the measurement of output is rendered obsolete by technological development. The case of the unemployed and precarious workers allows it to preserve a semblance of existence.

That is why a French group, the Association of the Unemployed and Precarious Workers, is demanding, in a wholly plausible and legitimate way, that persons employed on a precarious basis as temporary or casual workers should be given the right, during periods when wage labor is interrupted, to an income that remunerates them for remaining available for work. In exchange, they commit themselves to performing a certain annual amount of work, if it so happens that they are offered any. This is equivalent, in fact, to calling for a reduction in the working year and for the right to work in an intermittent fashion without any substantial reduction of income. The discontinuous nature of the wage relation is to be transformed into a new freedom instead of being suffered as a constraint imposed by management. There is nothing strange about such a demand. Until the 1910s, it was abnormal for a worker—particularly for a good craftworker—to work in a stable job the whole year long. For those workers, frequent job changes, unemployment, traveling, and casual work were all ways of preserving their independence both from management and from wage labor. That taste for change, for independence and autonomy, reappeared some time ago among a proportion of the work force that is too large to be dismissed as insignificant. These workers, most of them young, prefer temporary work to stable, full-time employment, as this leaves them free to engage in activities that are more fulfilling than most of those by which one can earn a living.

Keane: This distancing from work no doubt has its positive side. But it is important to point out that, in the OECD countries, between 70 and 90 percent of part-time workers, most of whom are in precarious forms of employment, are women between twenty-five and forty-four years old, employed in the service sector. For many of these women, working shortened hours means working a "double shift": unpaid work at home plus paid work—generally poorly paid—with no chance of career advancement. The result is that a great many women have much less free time and are more overworked than men.

Gorz: Quite so. It's doubly iniquitous and doubly scandalous.

In the first place, the economic system produces increasing wealth with a decreasing quantity of work. Yet it refuses to redistribute the work in such a way that everyone can work less and better without loss of income. It prefers to have a section of the population working full-time, another section unemployed, and a third, which is constantly growing in numbers, working a shortened day for reduced pay.

Furthermore, most full-time jobs are held by men and most jobs with reduced working hours by women. That is another scandal, which we shall only be rid of when paid working hours are reduced for everyone. If the normal working week were no more than thirty hours—which is the target of the Left and of trade unions in the Netherlands, Italy, and Germany—then the present sexual division of labor would lose its economic foundation and there would be no way to excuse it.

This is certainly the trend. First, an increasing proportion of young fathers are requesting shorter working hours or leave— even unpaid leave—in order to be able to look after their children. Four years ago, the figure was 12 percent in the United States. A year ago it was 26 percent, and half of American firms offer their male employees the option of working shorter hours. Second, almost half of French, German, and Swiss couples stay unmarried, and in half of these cases they don't live together. The children live with the mother, with the father, or with each in turn. This fundamentally changes the meaning of unpaid domestic labor. Women or men who live alone do their housework for themselves, not for the greater profit or comfort

of their partner. So as this trend continues, there is no longer any sense in asking society to recognize the social usefulness of household labor by paying wages for housework. However, this development lends a greater urgency and enhanced legitimacy to the demand for the right to paid parental leave, a sabbatical year, or other forms of reducing time at work.

This kind of right is often claimed on behalf of the "social usefulness" of the mother's (or father's) work in the home. The argument is that the social value of housework must be recognized as equal to the value of paid work. I don't agree with that approach, which takes as its basic criterion the individual's usefulness to society, because it implicitly denies the autonomy of the individual and the existence of his or her inalienable rights *upon* society. We must abandon the idea that society has priority and that individuals make themselves useful by reproducing it, and instead reverse the terms. Society will be better insofar as it acknowledges the rights of individuals to fulfill themselves and grants them the opportunities for such fulfillment. The right to motherhood, to fatherhood, to take care of one's body and one's habitat, to "look after oneself" and look after one's neighbor must be unconditional and privileged. It is on this basis that society will be created.

Keane: Isn't the extension of free time also a means of reducing overconsumption? The more commodities we consume, the more we need to work to buy them and the less time we have for other activities, including the activity of being citizens.

Gorz: Yes, and the opposite is true too: the more you work, the more you tend to consume commodities, but also to consume commodity services, since you don't have the time or energy to do things by and for yourself. The obligation to work full-time has been the key to economic growth in the affluent capitalist societies. The Swedish economist Gunnar Adler-Karlson was, I think, the first to say this in his book *The Unimportance of Full Employment.* If we could adjust our working time to the needs we really feel, how many hours would we work? But this possibility of "choosing our working hours" isn't offered to us. It would enable us to limit our consumption of commodities, which

has become an ecological imperative in the affluent nations. And the possibility of choosing our working hours will be all the greater as the normal weekly or annual working hours become shorter.

Keane: In *Ecology as Politics,* you adopt two contradictory points of view. On the one hand you say that the ecological approach is incompatible with capitalist rationality, and on the other you argue that capitalism will eventually accept ecological imperatives, just as it eventually accepted universal suffrage and the forty-hour week. Thus, according to you, these imperatives mustn't be ends in themselves for the Green movement. Why this ambiguity?

Gorz: The ecological movement can't be reduced to the demand that the environment be protected. If it is, its demands will end up sooner or later being taken on board by capitalism— and nothing will change. We shall have—we already have— ecobusiness and an ecoindustry, and we could have a techno-ecosphere, if not indeed technoecofascism as described in science fiction. Capitalism may develop a highly profitable ecobusiness, just as it developed a highly profitable arms industry, to meet public contracts. And in response to new pollution standards, it may better eliminate and recycle industrial waste products and adopt different, more capital-intensive technologies, at the cost of higher prices and increased inequalities. This is the direction in which we are going at the moment: the growing pauperization of the poor and the increasing affluence of the well-off.

Unlike what is called "environmentalism" in the Anglo-Saxon countries, political ecology does not confine itself to trying to reduce the impact of the existing system of production on the environment. It challenges the reasons behind the development of a certain number of technologies, products, and forms of consumption in the first place. These reasons are contained in the logic of capitalist accumulation: it has to be possible for increasing quantities of capital to be invested at a profit, and this requires the consumption of an increasing flow of commodities and commodity services. The population, therefore, has to be

induced to satisfy its needs through a maximum of consumption, and a maximum number of needs for commodity consumption have to be created. Now, many needs could be satisfied by a less intense flow of better, more durable products, and consumer needs themselves could be reduced by a more relaxed and convivial style of life that left more free time. We could live and work better by consuming less, provided that we consumed differently. It would not then be possible for technologies, social relations, our model of consumption, or our relation to nature to remain the same.

The "environmentalist" and "ecological" approaches are therefore fundamentally different from each other. The former imposes new constraints and new limitations on the free operation of economic rationality as developed by capitalism. But these constraints and limitations don't alter the basic tendency of the system, which is to extend the sphere of economic rationality and increase the value of rising amounts of capital. The ecological approach, in contrast, involves a paradigm shift, which may be summarized in the slogan "less but better." It aims to reduce the sphere in which economic rationality and commodity exchanges apply, and to subordinate it to nonquantifiable societal and cultural ends and to the free development of individuals. The ecological restructuring of the economy envisaged within the Left in Germany and the Netherlands and within the Italian extreme Left thus necessarily has an anticapitalist, socialist direction to it. Investment can no longer have economic growth as its goal, but only negative growth and an accompanying expansion of those activities not governed by monetary evaluation and the pursuit of maximum efficiency and profit.

Keane: The German "Greens" were the first to popularize the idea of a guaranteed social income or "universal grant." This idea is now making headway all over Europe, particularly in the Netherlands, where it is supported by all the Left movements, by some of the trade unions, and by many influential personalities. It is being debated in Italy and it has given rise in France to the creation of the "minimum insertion income." A guaranteed social income for everyone is regarded by many as a citizen's

right—the right to a "citizenship wage." It could also be the most important way of redistributing paid work fairly and reducing the length of working hours. Now, you have come out against such a formula on several occasions. You would rather have a system that guarantees every citizen a normal wage throughout his or her lifetime in exchange for performing over that lifetime a quantity of work, which would decrease and become more and more intermittent as social productivity increased. It is often held against you that, by linking the right to an income with the right to work, you are crucially linking the right to an income with an obligation to work. Isn't there a contradiction between an obligation of this kind and the break with the ideology of work that you advocate elsewhere?

Gorz: I consider utopian, in the bad sense of the term, ideal objectives that don't indicate new possibilities for emancipatory action. This is the critique I would make, as Jürgen Habermas does, of Hannah Arendt's disciples, who see the "citizenship wage" as a way to revive the ideal of the Greek polis. I see two fundamental defects in this universal-allowance idea.

The first is that an allowance of this kind, in exempting people from performing any paid work, fails to create a public space for noneconomic activities. Economic activity today occupies the public space to an exaggerated extent, and Arendt was right to wish to press it back, allowing more scope for political activities, activities that concern the "common good." It will not, however, be ousted from that space by paying an allowance to those who stay outside the economic sphere and thereby remain outside what is today the most important dimension of the public sphere. On the contrary, an allowance that exempts people from any work within the economic sphere will deepen the split within society. Economic activity will become the province of production-mad, profit-hungry individuals. They will tend to monopolize the public space and marginalize the nonworking recipients of state allowances, who will then be condemned to a life of private activities and social oblivion. If you want other activities to supplant work within the public space, then the importance of work has to be reduced through organized public action, which simultaneously opens

up the public space to activities whose ends are not economic and helps to establish such activities in that space. That is why, in my opinion, we have to come at the problem "from below," by reducing the number of working hours. And this has to be conceived not as a single measure but as a long-term, general policy, concerning both government and trade unions, and embodying an alternative view of civilization. Trade-union action—i.e., action by trade unions with a much broader conception of their role and, as argued by Negt in Germany and Trentin in Italy, a different structure—is indispensable if that objective is to be achieved. This is true, first, because only the (renovated) trade union can organize the population in the public space of work and open up that space to public activities outside the workplace, and second, because the shortening of working hours has to be worked out in concrete detail and applied through collective action and bargaining at all levels. A new "contract for society" has to be established so that social relations can be transformed. A universal allowance created by a law and paid out by an administrative agency would not have the same scope.

The right to work has to be understood in this context— as a *political* right of access to what is currently the chief activity within the public sphere and to the powers that access confers, in particular the power to participate in decisions relating to the organization of economic activity and its place in society. It is quite conceivable, of course, that the unemployed should take part, by rights, with their own associations, in the formulation of trade-union policy. But unemployment then has to be understood as a temporary and partial interruption of participation in economic activity and not as a choice not to participate in it at all. By opening up this right to nonparticipation, the universal-grant idea in fact creates two categories of citizen, and gives society the right to perpetuate forms of social exclusion.

The second defect of the universal grant can be seen if we approach the problem from the opposite angle. A certain quantity of work is essential for the existence of society and social individuals. That necessity is imposed by the nature of things, not by a social obligation. In the ancient polis,

economically necessary work was confined to the private sphere and reserved for women and slaves. The private sphere was the sphere of authoritarian constraint, whereas the public sphere was the sphere of free citizens, of men freed from the burden of necessity. The emancipation of the slaves reversed this type of political order. The equality and freedom of individuals now requires that necessary work be socially organized in the public sphere, where everyone participates. No one must bear the burden of necessity for the benefit of others, and no one, therefore, must be exempted from bearing his or her share of that burden. Now, the universal-grant idea opens up the right to exemption. It allows society not to concern itself with distributing the burden equitably. In so doing, out of idealism, it plays along with the ideology of work: it seems to consider work as an elective, optional activity, which can be reserved for those who like doing it. But the point is that work has to be done, whether we like it or not, and it is only by starting out from the recognition of its necessity that we can try to make it as pleasant and fulfilling as possible, to lessen its intensity and shorten its duration.

Admittedly, not all necessary work can be organized socially in the public sphere, nor should it be. There is a sphere within which individuals must belong to themselves and sovereignly produce themselves, free from all control and from social norms. This is the private sphere. Necessary work within that sphere cannot have the same status as work in the public sphere. I call this "work for oneself." It is ambivalent, being at once burdensome and gratifying, or each of these in turn, depending on the circumstances. Not doing such work means entrusting it to servants. It is mainly made up of all the various activities of self-maintenance. Such work will be less burdensome and more gratifying as free time is more abundant, on a daily, weekly, and yearly basis.

Keane: If working time is gradually reduced to the point where paid work becomes intermittent, what will people live on during the intervals between work? You have spoken of a guaranteed social income spread out over a lifetime, to be paid in exchange for a decreasing amount of work. But employers, and even a

large number of trade unions, will tell you that the cost of such a system would be beyond what the economy could bear.

Gorz: The six-day week and the eight-hour day were originally regarded as ruinous demands. The present social security system would have seemed completely unrealistic seventy years ago. At the beginning of the century, full-time employment meant working more than three thousand hours a year. In 1960, the figure was twenty-one hundred. In 1985, it was sixteen hundred hours, and yet this volume of work, which was 25 percent lower than the 1960 figure, produced a GNP two-and-a-half times higher. In his latest book, Jacques Delors points out that in 1946 a twenty-year-old wage-earner could expect to spend one-third of his or her waking life at work. By 1975, this had fallen to one-fourth, and today it is less than one-fifth. He adds that this development will continue, and that it should "give rise to other logics of production and exchange." In fact, if you consider the different types of leave from work, whether paid or covered by insurance, full-time work is already intermittent. There is no reason why we shouldn't gradually get back to an average of one thousand working hours a year—which was the norm in the eighteenth century—or twenty to thirty thousand hours a lifetime, enabling everyone successively to adopt several lifestyles, jobs, careers, or types of activity without ever ceasing to receive a full wage. We have to get used to thinking of free time as a major part of life, not as just the inferior time left over after work. It is the time in which paid work is done that has to become—and in fact already is—secondary in importance.

Keane: But if people are to be paid uninterruptedly for increasingly discontinuous work, what will force them to resume socially necessary activity after several months' or even one or two years' break? If people are actually to do the amount of work that entitles them to a guaranteed income during their lifetimes, won't a whole system of bureaucratic controls be needed? Won't people have to possess a logbook, as they did in Czechoslovakia, for example, recording the exact amount of work they have performed?

Gorz: Your pension fund already contains a record of the number of weeks and months you have worked and what you have earned over your lifetime. Instead of being paid from the age of fifty-five—or even fifty—onward for a period of complete inactivity that will continue until you die, why shouldn't you be entitled to spread out that economically—but not socially—inactive period over your life? It is no more difficult to manage by computer. A number of points is allocated for each working period, and these entitle you to a certain period of leave, paid on the basis of the average of what you have earned in your previous jobs. If you go too long without working, the computer sends you a letter warning you that you have only three months, say, to find work again. And the system could be combined with regulatory incentives. If, for some reason or other, there is a sudden need for nursing staff or bricklayers, the right to leave could be suspended and those on leave encouraged to work; they might, for example, be offered a higher number of points for going back to work. The Swedish economist Gösta Rehn was the first to propose a system of this kind, with incentives added, allowing people to take a kind of advance on their retirement at any age. One can imagine half a dozen other schemes and raise objections to each of them. I am not defending any particular system, but I am saying there is a need to imagine a way out of the "work-based society" toward a society in which activities performed for noneconomic ends—whether public or private, social or personal—will be preponderant.

Keane: But these will still have to be financed, since you yourself do not believe in a society without money in which everything would be free. This presupposes fiscal and monetary policy.

Gorz: That policy must reconcile three types of interest that appear to be contradictory: first, the legitimate interest of people who don't want their real incomes to fall when their working hours are reduced; second, the legitimate interest of enterprises, whether public or private, which can only be managed efficiently and with foresight if they know their real costs and are not made to pay people they don't actually need; third, the legitimate interest of society, which has to be able to

establish priorities and discourage certain forms of consumption and production by deterrent taxes similar to those that already exist, from which export products are exempt.

We have to conceive, then, a way of financing all this that does not burden either the incomes of working individuals or the manufacturing costs of enterprises. This is the case with taxes on consumption, of the VAT type, which could be very greatly increased on those industrial products whose relative prices are continually falling. These taxes would supply a fund that would pay people their incomes during nonworking periods. But you could also envisage having different types of money, for example, a "circulation money" that couldn't be hoarded, a "neighborhood money," for trading services, that could not circulate, etc. In short, "other logics of production and exchange," as Jacques Delors says.

A political strategy centered on the reduction of working hours may be the main lever with which we can shift the balance within society and put an end to the domination of the political sphere by the economic. And this would mean the extinction of capitalism.

Keane: Perhaps not. It might also lead to a post-Keynesian era that would leave privately controlled capital a significant role, albeit reduced by comparison with the previous period. Aren't you supposing that capitalism can be destroyed by stealth and that capitalists resemble old men on their deathbeds, ready to sign over their estates?

Gorz: I'm quite happy to accept what you call "a significant role, albeit reduced," for capital. That is precisely what is meant by the extinction of capital*ism*. We have to distinguish between capitalism and the logic of capital. Capitalism is a social system in which life, activities, the scale of values, and the aims of individuals and society are all dominated by relations subordinated to economic rationality and directed toward the valorization of capital. The logic of capital, by contrast, is the only form of pure economic rationality. There is no economically rational way to run an enterprise other than capitalist management. That is an obvious fact that everyone has

come to acknowledge. But it doesn't mean that all enterprises and activities have to obey capitalist management, or that the pure economic rationality such management represents must or even can take priority over all other considerations, at the level either of the enterprise or of society as a whole. The criterion of economic efficiency demands the pursuit of the greatest possible productivity per unit of (dead or live) labor. In practice, this means the pursuit of maximum profit. But this criterion is applicable only to a restricted area of what Marx called our "exchanges with nature." The application of the criterion of measurable productivity has, then, to be restricted by the application of criteria of a totally different kind. When these criteria win out over the logic of capital in public decision-making and individual behavior, and assign economic rationality the subordinate role of a means in the service of noneconomic ends, then we shall have gotten beyond capitalism to a different society, if not indeed a different civilization.

Of course, you might object that the capitalists will resist fiercely and their resistance will have to be overcome. How? By whom? This brings us back to the problem I mentioned a moment ago. There is a central conflict, but no central front; there are antagonisms similar to the class struggle, but no class capable of hegemony. Who got the better of the formidable political and financial power of the nuclear industry in Sweden, Austria, Switzerland, Germany, Italy? Who turned such things as the extinction of species, the destruction of the tropical rain forests, the hole in the ozone layer, global warming, the pollution of groundwater, industrial agriculture, and factory livestock farming into themes of a debate that confronts all political forces throughout Europe and that seems ready to lead not just to technocratic measures but to radical structural reforms?

There is a movement, a change; we're seeing transverse alliances that cut across class boundaries. Each of us knows some capitalist or other, a top manager in the chemical industry, for example, who is racked with doubt about what he is doing and wonders what his deathbed assessment of his life's work will be or what his great-grandchildren will think of him. Cultural

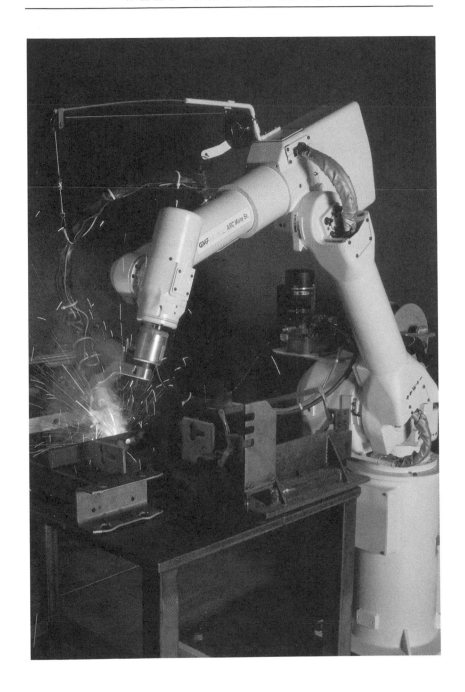

change and ideas have a force of their own, even on people whose interests they upset. Admittedly the managers of the capitalist mega-machine won't be converted spontaneously to ecological self-limitation and socialist democracy. But quite a few of them will be relieved and even prepared to cooperate when public pressure and legislators ask them to serve goals more defensible than merely maximizing profit to the detriment of people's health and the quality of life.

—Translated by Chris Turner in collaboration with André Gorz

Mutanabbi in Exile

*(Abu al-Tayyib al-Mutanabbi, the greatest of all
classical Arabic poets, moved from court to court
in Syria, Egypt, and Iraq, earning his living as a
panegyrist. He was murdered by robbers in 965.)*

In alien courts I melodied for bread
But now the sordid business of verse
Enjoins me to this dry, northern
Kingdom where disaffected ostriches
Snort at sundown and the prince
Idles the hours away with paradigms
In ancient grammar books.

A shabby gentility obscured my youth.
Poverty was a stench I couldn't scrub
And largesse smarted out of others' hands.
But language was immeasurable as shame
And burned in the beatific mouth of God
—He is exalted!—and now language flows
From my fingertips and from my quill
The way the spider tessellates its silk.

My heart is fringed with arrows like the sun
Or the chastened, wincing surface of a blade
Hammered in Damascus out of Indian steel.
My heart is like the chilly ramparts of cranes
Longing southward as the winter dawns.
But my lines still rustle lovely as the slide

Of rosaries of olive wood blessed by pilgrimage
Or the pages startled as acacia
In the whispering codices of the Law.

The moon enacts its faded casuistries
And there are thorn trees twisted like beggars
By the last stones of encampments, the dry
Dung of pack-animals, and thumam-grass
Stuffed in the fire-crevices. There I stopped
And all my pain swept over me
In that smooth-blown place.
How could such meager anonymous shreds
Summon remembrance in a spill of tears?
South of Aleppo, where the stony mesas gust
With desolation and the jackal-bitch whimpers
And snuffles in an unloved earth, my longing
Rang as hungry as the crows of winter.
The inkwell knows me, and the carven quill,
And the tense and crackling surfaces of parchment,
And swords and lances know me, and the strong horses,
And the night will remember me, and all empty places.

Egypt

When I traveled for the first time to Egypt, in 1989, I was amazed. The actuality of the place shattered all my expectations. Eternity takes form there. The ancient tombs and monuments retain their integrity and their stillness, which are only amplified by the crush of tourists and the chaotic energy of modern Egypt.

I was one more awed witness.

—Linda Connor

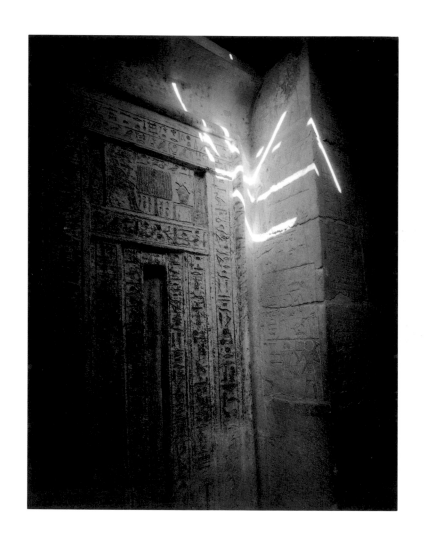

Egypt

p. 169 *Valley of the Queens, Egypt*

p. 170 *Osiris, Egypt*

p. 171 *Tomb and Pyramid, Giza, Egypt*

p. 172 *Tomb, Egypt*

p. 173 *Stone with Hieroglyphics, Egypt*

p. 174 *Guardians, Egypt*

p. 175 *Behind the Pyramids, Giza, Egypt*

p. 176 *Spirit Door, Egypt*

Days of Autumn

1

Dusty leaves cast their shadows, and the bee,
That ancient prophetess, now wordlessly
 Buzzing of the wide wilderness, believes
Those shadows cast by what will come to be.

2

The full, ripe silence where the grain was sown
The lingering sigh of tall grass lately mown,
 Rise from these tedious, ordinary fields:
Don't draw on outline, but take note of tone.

3

The day of the long days has shed its noon,
Lain nakedly, and now awaits the moon,
 Donning the orange veil that sunset draws
Across what will be long ago too soon.

4

August remembered autumn, but not old
December, as its shortening days unrolled.
 Heat waved away, in summery dismissal
The winter's now-long-buried pot of cold.

5

Fields; the late harvest standing still in sheaves:
Is it the rising of the wind that grieves
 My forest self, *mon* moi *longue d'Octobre*
Who sang before the falling of the leaves?

6

Cadences of familiar songs Can lie
In hiding here Where fields and open sky
 Declaim In prose, unchanted, clear, The texts
Left high and dry When the fall wind swept by.

7

"*Ist Sommer? Sommer* war," wrote Paul Celan.
Imperfect autumn lingers, and so on
 And so forth while we pause as the last song
Of one lost summer swims by like a swan.

8

At length, the hill of thought was undermined
By pain, tunneling through its hard and blind
 Rock, into which runs our advancing train,
Leaving the plain of fancies far behind.

9

Ah, for her I lost! for me whom I gave
Away to nothing! for all I could not save!
 The raving wind disperses in the oaks.
Light grieving slumps into a heavy grave.

10

No nova flaring in November, less
And less renewal as the trees undress:
 We shiver down past mere noon and its non-
Age, and its hopeless whiffs of agelessness.

11

Blood's shadow lay beneath the light green shade
The chestnut branches by the meadow made.
 The field of beets became a battlefield,
The plough's fair share fell to another blade.

12

Autumn's brood stripped by late November's rude
Whips, our decaying health last year renewed
 Our well-known bodies' growing oddness, the
Stupidity of our decrepitude.

13

Above my dimmed eyes the barn owl, below
The shivering mouse, and then—and so we go.
 The dark point of this nocturne's both what I
Believe I see and what I know I know.

14

It was the gray sidewalks which taught my feet
The truth of their particular concrete:
 All? not this general Being of the land;
The *Way?* not through the fields, but up the street.

15

The years of childhood days—extended fears,
Joys and anticipations: time and tears
 Contract their terms, which, in the Psalmist's phrase,
Have withered to the brief days of our years.

16

That bright, young person that I was, all prim
Exuberance, safe wonder, bridled vim:
 Ingrate! He never gave a damn for me.
I weep for what I could have done for him.

17

Shining in sunlight through the winter trees
These little brooks appear now as they freeze,
 At liberty to glitter, at long last
Recovered from fluidity's disease.

18

January. Epipromethean, or
Just plain two-faced? Here standing at the door
 Of the year, staring both in and out, he knows
What lies before him is what has gone before.

We Are Climbing Jacob's Ladder

From the window of a wandering Greyhound, Stuart Ressler gets his first look at the unmistakable I-state phenotype: the unvarying horizon, Siberian grain-wastes, endless acres of bread in embryo call to him like home. Schooled in the reductionist's golden rule, he sees in this Occam's razor-edge of emptiness a place at last vacant enough to provide the perfect control, a vast mat of maize and peas, Mendel's recovered Eden. Green at twenty-five, with Ph.D., he leaves the lab to enter the literal field.

The tedious bus haul catches him up on the literature. The *Journal of Molecular Biology* takes him into Indiana, where he acquires a seatmate whose disease of choice, obesity, spills over the armrest into Ressler's seat. When Ressler takes up the *National Academy Proceedings*, the huge stranger lets loose on the perils of reading. "My father could put away a Zane Grey in one afternoon, and it got him nowhere. You'd be wise to go easy on it." Ressler nods and twists his lips, but his seatmate persists. "What do?"

Quick decoding eliminates "Gesundheit" as an appropriate response. "I'm a geneticist."

"You fix women trouble? What I wouldn't do to trade places with you. Oh *brother*. What I wouldn't do."

Fortune extracts the man at Indianapolis, and the plague of companionship passes. When he is safely into Illinois, a half hour from his new life, organics lays a last ambush. A stream of tortoises possessed by mass instinct crawls across the highway in the twilight. Bottlenecked cars take turns gunning, crunching over the shells. The tortoise-trickle doesn't even waver. Ressler stares out the rear window as long as he can stomach it. For a hundred yards, the insane persistence of the parade holds him in fascinated disgust.

But Chelonia has nothing over primates. A similar drive brings Ressler out here. Four years before, a fellow first-year grad stormed into his dorm room waving the legendary Watson-Crick article in *Nature*. The awesome aperiodic double helix—with its seductive suggestion of encoded information assembling an entire organism—spread before him, wider than the American wilderness. The next day, he dropped his four-year investment in biophysiology to rush the frontier.

He pointed out to his astonished advisor how much solid preparation he already had for the curriculum change, how much carried over into molecular. The scale change would be a snap. Besides, all significant breakthroughs were made by novices free from vested interests. In six months of ferocious precocity, he'd made believers of everyone. Research schools singled him out, recruiting him even as he put the last touches on his thesis. Guided by heroic impatience, he chose the post-doc at Champaign-Urbana. Illinois could get him started the fastest. The game was afoot; a lab's a lab so long as it's antiseptic. Hunch, induction, and technique could put even an I-state on the map.

At twenty-five with no major contributions yet, he's under the gun. Miescher was twenty-five when he discovered DNA ninety years before. Watson was twenty-four. If the symptoms of breakthrough don't show by thirty, forget it: throw in the lab coat, get an industry job. Research—in America in '57— is no country for old men. Sure, his dissertation was a minor tour de force, but it just juggled ideas evident to anyone paying attention. Now he must mint, in his new lab crucible, hard currency.

He acclimates instantly to the box houses, orthogonal blocks, and infinite corn—parallel plowcuts running to the horizon.

Stagnant backwaters are the most fecund. He needs only a supply of pipettes and a place to spread his bed. Stepping off the bus into the greasy station, he accredits downtown, shoos off the soliciting cab, walks to campus. All significant discoveries are made on foot. The squares of his adopted town bear ingenious names: numbers, states, presidents, and the trees slaughtered to make way for them. Streets swell with white wood houses, diners, five-and-dimes. A church pokes a Pentecostal finger at the nimbus laid over it, its promotional postboard asking, "Can the Guests Morn When the Bridegroom Be With Them?," the *u* deleted in point mutation. The rows lining each street seem so many complementary, self-replicating pairs—the fastest-breaking metaphor of the '50s. In minutes, Ressler forgets the seaboard, the flattened eastern affect of his childhood. He settles into this emptiness like a symbiotic bacterium in the belly of his host.

On campus, a superannuated department secretary predating fruit flies scrapes him up a place in the old army barracks, reprieved from destruction until veterans stop pouring back to school on the GI Bill. Stuart, who missed the world crisis by enough years to think that GI Bills come from internists for services rendered, also scabbed out of Korea on dissertation deferral. His thesis, a magic bullet as explosive as any gunner's, drafts him into another campaign. Military digs, then, seem fitting: vicarious enlistment. He takes possession of one end of a long, single-story, tar-paper shack in a shanty called Stadium Terrace. He delights in discovering that his cell number, K-53-C, encodes his precise locus within the village.

Cursory inspection turns up a ratty bunk, a gas stove, half a black-and-white print of James Dean with head on steering wheel, and a box of cereal with both flakes and enclosed coupon devoured by red ants. He needs nothing more. He unpacks his worldly goods: a tartan suitcase of second-hand clothes and a tote bag crammed with journals. Social rounds can wait. After a perfunctory trip to the convenience grocery, he holes up in the barracks for a week. Days he toys with the coding problem, and evenings he sits on a lawn chair staring at the wedge-shaped shelter signs plastered over the stadium across the way. For dinner, tomato juice without gin—alcohol is a trace mutagen.

He remains horizontal for days, boning up on the coding problem, resisting the temptation to indulge in premature cracking. He must consolidate, gather strength, quiet his mind, assemble the tools, await, without expecting, the visit of insight, that rare, most skittish creature. But before it can alight, the outside world flank-attacks him through the mail. A letter appears in his box, his first communiqué since hitting Illinois:

July 16, 1957

Dear Stu,

 Heard you're in town and hope you're not waiting for official commencement of the fellowship to drop by. We could use you in the Blue Sky sessions if nowhere else. No one's doing much biology at the moment; too much excitement in the air. Right now we're all thinking linguistics. Oh for a spark of Aha! By the way, Charlene and I are having the team over for dinner and cards or something next Thursday. Do come. We'll have the get-together in your honor, if that's what it takes.

Yours,
Karl Ulrich

P.S. Review *Adv Biol* 4:23 if you haven't done so recently, and let me know Thursday if you think Gamow's right in discarding the diamond code. I never liked the layout: too pretty. But too convenient if the whole pattern just coiled up and blew away.

Ressler has met his new boss only through the journals. Prolific, the man is to trees what Bill Cody was to buffalo. Ulrich, at fifty-two (Ressler's age transposed), is Illinois's grand old molecular man and the guiding spirit behind Cyfer, the mixed team of microbiologists, chemists, and geneticists who induct Ressler as new recruit. Ressler tracks the article down in the university library. The stacks, among the largest in the country, also bear the ubiquitous orange-and-black civil-defense pie wedges. He doubts that four floors of masonry would survive an airburst. And using the library as a fallout shelter until the renovated landscape returned to safe levels of radiation would require keeping survivors alive for weeks on cellulose alone.

 Nevertheless, this homage to Dewey Decimal is the most impressive monument America's breadbasket has yet shown him. Several million volumes colonize ten floors of catwalks

and twisting alleys. If the stink of binding paste didn't offend, Ressler would go AWOL from the barracks and set up his two pieces of luggage here. A sadly vindicating tour reveals an 824 untouched since Henry James died. Humanities have clearly slid into the terminally curatorial, forsaking claim to knowledge. By cytotropic sixth sense, Ressler finds his niche-to-be, 575, tucked away in a grotto deep in the spelunkers' recesses. This rarefied branch of a specialized discipline, barely extant a decade back, now rates several shelves, swelling by the hour.

At any other time, he'd be hopelessly waylaid by 1930s unemployment lists, turn-of-the-century political tracts, hundred-year-old sets of symphony programs. This comprehensive map, striving for isomorphy with the outside world, provokes his browser's awe. But commissioned, Stuart goes straight to the target periodical. He's read Gamow on the code—one of the first formal attacks on how DNA might imbed protein-plans. But best review the physicist's retraction; it's likely to be of more use at Ulrich's soiree than the latest Fats Domino. *Advanced Biology* 4:23 slips off the shelf suspiciously, plops open to the article in question, where a penciled scrawl near the title reads:

JHB SZI HVA OLP GVX IKZ XHO DBN ZRU ALW WKH TVI HQQ BTI VSR

EP

His brain stem throbs with the lure of this adept's sport, text trapped in nonsense, tapping impulses fiercer than the urge to pile up cars or cure the forbidding loneliness of women. The sanctioned desires of twenty-five—warm breasts and cold chrome—are mere substitutes, garbled misreadings of the *real* pull. All longing converges on this mystery, the unraveling of secret spaces, the suggestion that the world's valence lies just behind a scrambled facade. Cryptography alone reaches beneath the cheat of surfaces. This puzzle—clearly planted for his benefit—this chase, this unscrambling, waiting, working, worrying the breath-burst moment when irrefutable plaintext explanation descends: this (the cadence of his thought straying dangerously close to Protestant hymnody) is the reason why awareness itself evolved out of inert earth.

Experiment per se has never carried any special appeal; rare

steak aside, Ressler has never enjoyed cutting into any genus higher than *Anura*. But *naming* the transaction: that is the cold addiction. He sets to work on the pencil smudges. "EP," the closing, sole duple: perhaps the initials of his antagonist? He tries a few translations before hitting a simple relation. *P* to *U* is a jump of five letters; *E* to *K*, a jump of six. An incremental substitution cipher—a reasonable, reversible garbling scheme. Seven to the final *R* yields *Y*. Eight to the *S*, going around the horn, arrives at *A*. The last triplet comes out "day": payoff. The rest is brute counting. Soon the shell cracks and sense seeps through:

IFY OUC ANR EAD THI STH ENT HEP ART YIS REA LLY WED NES DAY
KU

A clear return to native tongue. Grouping by threes is Ulrich's hat-tip to the prevailing idea that the unit in the genetic code is a triplet of bases. Regrouping reveals all.

Ressler passes the rite of hidden passages, wins his first glimpse of the new boss. The path from discovery to tinkering to inspiration to solution takes place outside time. Returning to the deck entrance, he discovers that he has narrowly missed being locked in the stacks overnight. Only when he is safely back at the barracks, flat out on the bunk in K-53-C, sipping tomatoes and savoring his victory, does he realize that he's forgotten to glance at the article Dr. Ulrich asked him to review.

Stuart arrives at the Ulrich doorstoop on the revealed Wednesday, groomed for the occasion. The chief ushers him in to the party with a "Good job." Ressler, last to arrive, uncomfortable in a newly purchased suit, presents his host with a box of chocolates filled with greenish fungi. Suit and gift are both miscalculations; soon he'll be unable to go out in public at all, so completely has he botched the social code in his haste to crack the genetic.

He makes the rounds, meets his labmates. Tooney Blake, a youthful forty, is at the piano doing a terrifyingly down-tempo cover of "Let's Call the Whole Thing Off." Only he's missed the point: "Potato, potato, tomato, tomato," each pair pronounced exactly the same. A gracious woman doing an

uncanny Eleanor Roosevelt impersonation, Dr. Toveh Botkin stands by in great pain, waiting for the promised formal feeling to come. Her accent reveals her as one of those brilliant Central Europeans lured away from the Russians in '45 by democracy and cash. Judging by Dr. Botkin's bearing, the soiree is soul-toughening purgatory. She says as much in her first sentence, declaring with the tact of convoluted syntax that the machine that enabled Beethoven's Diabelli apotheosis had been a sacred instrument to her until a few moments before. Ressler nods, with nary a clue.

Joe Lovering sits on a sofa noisily denying that he is now or has ever been a member of this or any party. He and Jeanette Koss, both near thirty, discuss some political bomb that Ressler lost track of in grad school. Daniel Woytowich, senior Cyfer member with Ulrich and Botkin, sits in the corner, his head wrapped in Pyrex eyeglasses, watching a rabbit-eared set broadcast Gary Moore's "I've Got a Secret." The show is interrupted by a news flash: scientists have succeeded in creating today's modern aspirin: fast, faster, fastest, the Ferrari of the gastrointestinal LeMans. "Last year's aspirin only *killed* the headache . . ." Woytowich tells Ressler the panelist's secret: by marrying the mother of his father's second wife, he's become his own grandpa.

How can so human a collection hope to penetrate its own blueprint? The code must certainly be more ingenious than this crew, its proud creation. Ressler knows Cyfer's considerable collective intelligence from their published track record. He *needs* them, their specific expertise in cytology, biochemistry, ontogeny. Yet they sing, watch prime time, talk politics. Incredible comedown, awful circularity: no one to reveal us to ourselves but us.

The welcome-aboard party—easily his most nightmarish evening out since the prom—leaves Ressler in need of a purgative. He makes his first visit downtown since the bus pulled in. There he indulges in an act against type by buying something. Spending money has never been a problem; he's never been one to form emotional bonds with crinkled, septic bits of safety paper. But since his late teens he's never owned anything more than he could carry out of the country on short notice. Now,

in less than a month, he's already saddled himself with dishes, shelves, even a chicken-wire sculpture that charitably passes for a chair.

He buys a record player that folds up into a box with a handle, its color a pink that has been coaxed out of the spectrum by suspect means. He is sold by a matching pink polyethylene ballerina that snaps onto the spindle and pirouettes slavishly at 78, 45, 33⅓, and—whatever happened to 16?—16. Amusical, he inherited what is physiologically referred to as a tin ear. His father carried the tone-deaf gene, forever going about the house delivering a toneless version of "Get Out and Get Under." A deeper discomfort with harmony leaves Ressler not only ignorant of music but deeply distrustful of it. Pitch-writing is a language obscure, amorphous, ambiguous—a dialect just beyond paraphrase. Fast and loud is more exciting than slow and quiet. The rest is silence.

He needs, without knowing it, those old Renaissance formulas equating C-sharp minor with longing, sudden modulation to E with a glimpse of heaven. How dare an obnoxious greaser four years younger than he turn the Civil War tune "Aura Lee" into the hit-parade standard "Love Me Tender," without a word of concern for the underpinning chordal message? Either this language *has no content*, or tonal tastes have festered for 115 years. Neither prospect is palatable.

He has trouble selecting tunes to keep the ballerina dancing, and Olga herself remains noncommittal. At length, he grabs an anthology called *Summer Slumber Party*, the bobby-soxer behind the pillow, center cover, reminding him of a woman he dated in college. With the assistance of an informed sales clerk, he buys two other primers: Britten's *Young Person's Guide to the Orchestra* and *Leitmotifs from Wagner's "Ring."* The latter, still politically suspect, appeals to him because of the liner description: a story told in a book-code of memorable riffs. One of these discs might contain his tonal Rosetta. To round out his disc library, in the spirit of Separate Can Never Be Equal, and knowing the tunes from his father, he buys an album of spirituals by Paul Robeson.

A summer night, the last before his marriage to experiment, and Ressler spends the dark, warm hours soaking in the

evangelical minister's voice spreading spirituals from K-53-C onto Stadium Terrace's lawn. Robeson sings, "Sometimes it causes me to wonder. Ah, sometimes." The sound ambushes Ressler, slack in his lawn chair. The waves continue east at 1,134 feet per second, arriving in D.C. later that evening. He hears the phrase knock at John Foster Dulles's window as the secretary of state prepares for bed. Dulles curses, shouts for this blackfella to leave him be. He's promised to return Ol' Man River's passport as soon as Robeson returns the 1952 International Stalin Peace Prize. Last year Dulles told a *Life* reporter that a man scared to go all the way to the brink is lost. Brinkmanship is now the going word. Dulles, hands full with the Suez and Syria, his troops already destined for Lebanon, shaken by the runaway slave's son singing "Jordan River chilly and cold," shouts out the window of the State Department at Ressler to turn the volume down and have a little respect, forgetting, under stress of the brink, that democracy is the privilege of being unable to escape the next man's freedom of speakers.

Ressler, a thousand miles west, listens to the blackfella go on to sing, in resonant bass, the great ascent up Jacob's ladder. Every rung—now the steps of the four nucleotides up the spiral DNA staircase—goes higher and higher. On the darkened barracks lawn, gathering strength for the work he owes the world, he feels his peace turn to a sadness so overpowering that, before he can interpret it, tears seep out his ducts on underground springs. Avuncular defective lachrymal gland, until this moment masked, flushed by the deep voice, the simplicity of the tune, the hopeless hope of words in a world where buildings declare themselves safe radiation havens, or just this still spring night in a featureless town. Spontaneous seep of gland for a race capable of grabbing the next rung while simultaneously leaping for the beloved brink. Or purely somatic epiphenomenon: Robeson hits a note, springs a sequence that triggers solute; everything else lies outside measure. Deeply enfolded, the tune attaches to the night's lateness, and suddenly the song is real. Ah! sometimes it causes me to wonder. Sometimes. There on the lawn, on the eve of uncovering the precise, testable tape that will change the way life conceives itself, he feels the first seduction of music, his own pitiful compulsion for forward motion, the

insistence that we sing ourselves into a further place. All the while the runaway slave's son intones:

> We are climbing Jacob's ladder
> We are climbing Jacob's ladder
> We are climbing Jacob's ladder
> We're soldiers of the Cross.

Rearguard, he runs through the lexical combinations biology reserves for that five-letter word: cross stain, hair cross, Ranvier's cross, crossbreed, cross-firing, crossing-over, cross-matching, sensory crossway.

> Every rung goes higher and higher
> Every rung goes higher and higher
> Every rung goes higher and higher
> We're soldiers of the Cross.

To this cross list, he adds the crucial test cross, the only way to tell how he and the bass are related, to locate the miscegenation linking them. Then he hits on it, the mark, the label for the spiritual's crucifix, the deep, reluctant cross Robeson soldiers under. Anatomical term: crux of the heart.

If the great debate of the '40s raged over which macro-molecule carried hereditary material, and if in the early '50s the fight was over nucleic acid structure, *the* scientific contention of 1957 is the one Ressler walks into on his first day in the lab. A working relationship with microorganisms made him bathe this morning before leaving the barracks. Regular dawn dunking gives him time for undirected reflection; like Luther's, his best insights arrive in proximity to porcelain. But drying his hair before setting off is time lost to superfluity. The omission puts him into the scientific cross hairs.

While he unpacks his glassware and sets up a cot in a storage room, Jeanette Koss passes his counter and lays a discreet hand on his. The contact startles Stuart; real skin rubbing the fur of his arm—so long has he been without—cuts like an accusation. Dr. Koss whispers, "If Blake or Lovering catch sight of you like this, your year is ruined."

In the same soft confidence, she spells out how Lovering, her soiree sparring partner, and Blake, the pianist of less than

Gershwinning ways, are locked in dispute about the hazards of going outside with a wet head. The two scientists share commensurate views on the coding problem. But on this matter they are bitterly bipolar. Blake devotes himself to a systematic destruction of the old wives' hypothesis linking wet hair to open season for viruses. For the last month he's immersed his head twice daily before going outside. Lovering, on the other hand, not only maintains bone-dry hair at all times but even now, late July, keeps up a steady regimen of preventive tonics. "You see," Koss explains, releasing Ressler from her touch, "they have no control group. If they catch you like this, you're It."

To date, he's lain low in the exchange between lab partners Niki and Ike. But his colleagues in deciphering have brought the Cold War home. Best avoid getting caught in the draft. Ressler thanks Dr. Koss for the caveat, but that's not sufficient. She produces a supply-room towel, and insists on wrapping his head in the fabric. Before he collects the presence of mind to object, she is rubbing him gently but briskly from crown to nape of neck. Buried memory shoots up through his scalp: his mother preparing him for church, a wedding or funeral. The wince of somatic recall—thumb moistened with saliva rubbing raw the skin behind his ears. The woman—married as they come—pinches his head into sweet pain. Koss smoothes back his hair, combs it, smiles, and crosses the room to resume her work with the vernier scales. In a minute, it's as if nothing out of the ordinary has happened; in two, Ressler's skin forgets the contact.

Ulrich's note was right; the lab is between measurements. The group is on extended leave from titrations, slide-stains, partition chromatography. They are after a transcription *axiom*. For the link between nucleotide sequences and protein synthesis to be determined experimentally, Cyfer must first play with shape, suspected inner symmetries. They are up against not so much the chemistry of biology as the grammar of it. Molecular genetics has a first shot at bridging the gap, grounding organic complexity in fundamental arithmetic. Ulrich has called an informal moratorium to assimilate the lightning experimental results of recent months and formalize Cyfer's understanding of the symbolic logic that genetics has stumbled on. A time for pure

speculation. Ressler's first day at school is a day to indulge in that old arbiter and sworn enemy of experiment: human reason.

Cyfer—for Cytology Ferment, although they aren't strictly in the wine business—is the catchiest name in the hard sciences since Bill Haley and the Comets. The sobriquet even gives them an edge with grants. But the name stands for a strange brew of personalities. Botkin bicycles up on a machine that took her on prewar pilgrimages to Bayreuth. Blake enters, abstractedly patting empty pockets everywhere on his person. Ulrich pulls into the department parking lot in a VW bearing the plate E COLI. When all are present and accounted for, Ressler joins his maiden Blue Sky session. The informal brainstorming gets underway, everyone tossing out abstracts of articles and volunteering to review others for the following week. Soon talk wanders onto topics that leave them sounding more like a clutch of cabalists.

From their predecessors—pylons in the vast, incomplete suspension bridge between the inanimate atom and the world ecoweb—Cyfer inherits a list of numbers it must arrange into a magic square. An alphabet of four nucleotide letters that, grouped into trinities, must produce a vocabulary of sixty-four different words. These three-letter words spell out immense miracle-sentences translated into a tongue of twenty amino acid actants. Cyfer shoots the blue, welding together these incunabula into a new gnosticism.

In a few minutes Lovering races from embracing the newest fad in punctuation to discarding it wholesale in favor of a newer, improved flyer. Woytowich, incredibly, is the last of the old guard to refuse the Watson-Crick model. His static-sparking comments reject the helix. He declares, in a folksy singsong tailored to get on everyone's nerves, "Too simple to be all there is." Whenever anyone says anything remotely lucid, Woyty shakes his head sadly and says, "We're overlooking something here. We're talking the big L, after all."

Ulrich is a bright spot in the painful group grope toward microunderstanding. He runs the session as a benevolent dictator, neither encouraging nor condescending, following the time-tested path to discovery: intellect proposes and measurement disposes. He fills the chalkboard with As, Ts, Gs, Cs, unzipping helices, decoding boxes, templates, diamonds, triangles, every

model short of hex signs. To one beautiful scheme that reveals a flaw when it rolls belly-up against experimental evidence, the chief shakes his head and pronounces stoically, "So goes poetry. Shipwrecked on shoals of fact."

The members compete to win the next stroke of praise. Ulrich makes them each sense that all of their names will appear on the resulting paper. Still, Ressler declines to put forth his private bias on how to begin cracking the coding problem. Reticence is not an issue, or fear of bruised ego. In his freshman session at the public trading post, the small crystal of clarity he now possesses might get lost in the hypothesizing. In a few weeks, after he learns the ropes, he'll lay out his vein, the method so new that he himself can't formulate it yet.

As Ulrich smoothly wraps up the Blue Sky session before it turns to Gray and Partly Cloudy, someone slips Ressler a note. More spectral number theory, a spidery, nineteenth-century hand.

> Dr. Ressler—
> Dismissals of verse notwithstanding, Fearless Leader harbors a closet predisposition to literature. I'll wager Ulrich has contracted Poe's Gold Bug. Communicable, I gather. J.K.

The syntax is the sequel to his earlier exercise in cryptography. But this note, on second reading, makes at least marginal sense. No need for letter substitution. Yet the words resist ultimate understanding. It doesn't occur to him, as the session breaks up, to ask JK herself what she means. He watches her leave the room and looks again at the note, the first he's received in twenty years of school. Dr. Koss glides across the lab and out the door. Monk Mendel's chief lesson returns from first-year genetics: that rift between genotype and phenotype. Surfaces lie.

At night, back in his bachelor and still unfurnished flat, Ressler lies in his bunk, wrapped in the barracks walls, the cradling vacancy of his adopted town. The day's stimulation prevents sleep. He runs through the proposed structure, which is entrancing all biology except Woytowich and a few lone holdouts. The spiral molecular staircase—two paired railings sinuously twisting around one another, eternally unmeeting snakes caught in a caduceus—becomes, in his fueled brain,

the stairs of Robeson's spiritual: Jacob's ladder, the two-lane highway to higher kingdoms. Angels descending and ascending in two solid, frozen, opposing columns. Four kinds of angel twist along the golden stairs—bright angels and dark, of both sexes. Four angel varieties freeze in two adjacent queues up and down the staircase, each stuck on a step that it shares with its exact counterpart. Every bright man opposite a dark woman. Every bright woman, a dark man. Fitful in his bunk, in the dark, in the unappeasable model-making urge. Four angel varieties to signify DNA's four bases: thymine, cytosine, adenine, and guanine. Jacob's helical staircase ladder conjured out of a single strand of nucleic acid.

How indispensable models have been to date. Watson and Crick did the trick with tin shapes, interlocking jigsawed pieces that refused to combine in any configuration consistent with the data except the spiral staircase. The great Pauling's snips of accordion paper, now an industry legend, were an industry joke until laughter was hushed by repeated success. Pauling's offspring—molecular spheres and dowels—pop up in classrooms, raising a race of clear-eyed students whose innovative exhalations already warm Ressler's neck. All the models agree: life science, to advance at all, cannot start with big and hope to pull it apart into underpinning little. It must begin with the constituents and tease them into a structure consistent with observation. Cyfer needs a model as simple and labile as baby blocks, a breathtaking Tinkertoy indistinguishable from the thing it imitates.

Four years ago Ressler, along with every other hapless haplotype, noticed that the double-spiral staircase embodied two identical informational queues. The ascending angel order complements the descending stream. Wholly redundant, each angel sequence can be entirely re-created from the other. Bright men, dark men, bright women, dark women: each half of a pair uniquely mated, each half of the staircase bearing the same message. There it was in Crick and Watson's tantalizing summary: "It has not escaped our notice that the specific pairing we have postulated immediately suggests a possible copying mechanism for the genetic material." The angel files in each half-stair must somehow be capable of latching onto

their proper mates out of the angelic bouillabaisse. Chemical lightning, sundering the staircase down its middle, unzipping it, creates two severed parades, each capable of re-creating the entire, original ladder. Ressler, in his bunk, has the wind sucked out of him by the ingenuity, the *rightness* of it: a long molecular chain, stupefyingly massive but obeying only chemical requirements, somehow lucks upon viability—the fundamental, self-replicating machine.

Stairway replication, an inanimate molecule's ability to double, is just the surface of the proliferate miracle. Somehow, incomprehensibly tortuously simply, coded in permutations of four bases alone, is all the sequence needed to conduct the full angel choir. On this dream of spiral ladders, he lulls himself into brief, shallow sleep. Rest does not last long, nor does he wake refreshed. He is back in the stacks at opening, armed with the tip-off Jeanette Koss has passed him. He came to Illinois to crack the nucleic code. To date the only triplets he's gone up against are Dewey Decimal. He looks up her clue in the card catalogue: Poe's "The Gold Bug." Mystery, suspense: a story in a thousand anthologies. It's been years since he's read any fiction except the Oppenheimer charges. But the library jump-table leads him to 813 as easily as if he were a regular.

Squatting between two metal shelves, Ressler loses himself in the adventure. Discovery—a piece of heated parchment reveals secret writing. Pictograph of baby goat identifies author as Captain Kidd, language of cipher as English. Simple letter frequency and word-pattern trick leads scholar to pirate's treasure. But directions to treasure are themselves a coded algorithm for unburying. Two men and blackfella servant, applying human ingenuity, measured paces, and plumb line, crack third-level mystery and uncover wealth beyond wildest dreams. Only at the story's end does he emerge, shake off the fictional spell. "Gold Bug" is the ticket all right; he's come to the right place.

If he understands Dr. Koss's warning, Ulrich may be in danger of confusing the *message* of base-string sequences with their translation *mechanism*. Bulling through frequency counts and base-order mapping, searching the impenetrable archive of nucleic rungs, will never reveal a simple correspondence rule

equating sequences with hair color, hand length, texture of skin. The game is immensely bigger; much more than gene-reading is at stake. To search for sequence-substitution, to pan for genetic gold bugs, would be tantamount to learning a foreign language armed with only a translating dictionary. That way will lead no further than a refinement of Morgan's endless *Drosophila* generations: chromosome bump X produces white eyes. A swap of one name for the other, no more than a means of reading individual messages without ever getting fluent in the mother tongue.

The catch they are after is not what a particular string of DNA says, but how it says it. For the first time, they might do more than wedge open the door. They must throw wide open the means of molecular articulation, master, with the fluency of native speakers, a language sufficiently complex and flexible to speak into existence the inconceivable commodity of self-speaking. The treasure in Poe's tale is not the buried gold but the cryptographer's flicker of insight, the trick, the linguistic key to unlocking not just the map at hand but any secret writing. Ressler must bring the team to see that they are up against something considerably larger than the pleasures of the Sunday cross-word, fitting a few letters into empty boxes. Not the limited game of translation but the game rules themselves. Sprawled between the girders of the 800s, in the summer of his twenty-fifth year, he gets his first hint of the word game he is up against. He must latch onto a language that can articulate its own axioms, a technique that can generate—in the effortless idiom it models—endlessly extensible four-letter synonyms for Life.

A knock at the barracks on another summer's evening, and Ressler hasn't a clue as to who it is. It can't be Dulles complaining about the noise; Ressler hasn't played Robeson for days. He throws the door open. Out where the welcome mat should be, incomprehensibly, stands short-sleeved, full-bodied Dr. Koss. Jeanette enters. Ressler, agape, neither prevents nor invites her. Her eyes trace an astonished arc over the monkish sparsity of the room. Only when she leans against a wall in a girlish slump does he collect himself. "What in the world are *you* doing here?"

She takes the Ur–punch line, jutting one arm over her head and slithering a side step. "The samba." Slowly, sadly, she sings, "When you can't reproduce 'cause you've lost all your juice, it's your birthday," to the tune of "That's Amore," inflicting no apparent damage on the sense of the chord progressions. She stops and examines Ressler, as if the burden of explanation rests on him.

"But it's not my birthday. Not yet." He feels his idiocy the instant he objects.

"No? Damn! And all the numerology worked out perfectly! I guess it's back to triplet coding. Here. I brought you a present anyway." She holds out a wrapped phonograph record tentatively, reluctant to give it up. Not knowing what else to do, Ressler unwraps it. It's a two-year-old recording of Bach's *Goldberg Variations* in a debut performance by a pianist who has the bad taste to be both as Canadian as Avery and younger than Ressler. "I'm sorry if the surface is ground to death. But I thought you deserved something better in life than bobby-soxers and Britten."

Ressler flinches at Koss's inside knowledge. He stands paralyzed, unable to extricate himself. "I don't understand. What is this?"

"It's a *record,*" she replies, with a pouty, apologetic smile at having to do all the vaudeville. "You put it on that machine and music comes out." She lowers her arm, still thrust in pseudo-samba, and sits cross-legged on the floor. She tilts her head and lets her face go sunbather slack. Ressler considers his options: deterrence has failed, and it is too late for a preemptive strike. He goes to the phono; for the first time since he bought her, Olga spins without suggestion of complicity. He removes the record from its worn cardboard, with difficulty finding side one. "Is your husband dropping by, too?" He tries for a neutral lilt.

"My husband doesn't care much for music. What Mr. Koss has no interest in could fill symposia." She faces him, equal parts coy and ashamed. His first good look at her: she is more juvenile, lighter than in profile. Suddenly she gesticulates for him to hurry and get the music on: Why else do you think I've come all the way here?

Nothing to do except release track one. He touches the

needle to the Goldberg aria. The bare octave, the simplicity of the unfolding triad, initiate a process that will mutate his insides for life. Transparent tones, surprising his mind in precisely the right state of confusion and readiness, suggest an urgent, private, concealed message. The pleasure of harmony— subtle, statistical sequence of expectation and release—he can only dimly feel. But the first measure announces a plan of heartbreaking proportions. What he fails to learn from these notes tonight will lodge in his lungs until they stop moving.

If the night is complete and the train of notes advances with certainty, even formal symmetry will grow as inevitably as a living thing. The fragmented melody, the decorated trickle coming from the speakers, the lights across the dark yard (so many ships' distress signals), the pile of slip-delineated journals swelling in the corner like an unassailable fairy-tale hill of glass, the foreign woman sitting on the floor not three meters away: everything aims this moment, indistinguishable and arbitrary, at his heart. This fluke, beautiful assortment: they are here alone. Certainly a message; the sentient musical line makes that explicit. A messenger, undeniably, at the keys. But no sender. No sponsor. Only notes, vertically perfect, horizontally inevitable.

Prompted by the aria's first octave, he at once looks through an electron microscope at a moment he will never afterwards succeed in re-creating. How can he *say* what he hears? He hears a melody (it can't quite be called that), ornamented, sighing its stately, frilly way into timeless irrelevance. He hears something else, something substantial, underneath the period piece: a bass line as patterned as the orbit of seasons, fueled by the same self-burning as the core of a star.

While the right hand tentatively ascends and turns, the left descends in nothing more ingenious than a major scale. What could be simpler? Four scale-steps descend from Do, answered by three rising tones before a temporary return home. The aria has traveled only eight measures, but Ressler comes far further. He skids across epochs, shaking time loose. The bass line insinuates itself through the most unassuming thirty-two measures imaginable: a third group of four notes is answered by a fourth, these eight together asserting a meta-echo to the initial

eight. This four-by-four mega-measure is in turn answered by a further sixteen—a perfect hierarchy where each internal rung is reflected at a higher level. A pulse, a row of tones, a magic square sprung from four letters: its Pythagorean perfection holds the hint of proliferation, a celestial blowout of uncountable possibilities.

The man, until this moment incapable of hearing that every song on *Summer Slumber Party* derives from the same I-IV-V progression as "Red River Valley," can hear in this spare pattern potential beyond telling: answers and calls, inversions, oppositions, expansions, contractions, dissonances, resolutions. He hears all these hiding in a tune so simple it cannot in truth even be called a tune. And the variations haven't begun yet.

How can a haphazard nubbiness of grooves pressed in synthetic polymer, read and converted into equivalent electric current, passed in turn through an electromagnet that excites speaker paper, sucking it back and forth in a pulsing wave that sets up a sympathetic vibration in thin skin membrane tickling electrical nerve-bursts, simulate not only all the instruments of the orchestra but this most cerebrally self-contained device, the hammer-struck, vibrating string? God only knows what those string vibrations themselves code for. But the pattern means something, he's sure. And if he lets what these notes conceal fall back into the obscurity they have momentarily raised themselves from, a tract of unsuspected signal will disappear, vanish along with this woman when she stands up to leave.

Underneath the graceful aria's surface is a skeleton, a stripped-down fragment, a moment not even a moment, a melody not yet the essential one. The real melody, the one that will pass with that trivial bass line through thirty wildly varying but constant mutations, is the accompaniment of desire and remorse, Ressler and Koss alone in this room. That bass is a mere crystal, periodic, irregular, growing in both directions, back into the imprecision of memory and forward, in a rush of premonition, into the logical consequence of its opening phrases, unsuspected adulthood. At the center of that spiral architecture of harmony, *this* moment leaves its fossil impression: a man and a woman, unwitting particulars of a species frozen forever in the stillness before the historical calamity that will finish

and preserve them, pressed in stratigraphy, here against the bare floor.

Tone-deaf, he hears, he is inside it. In its final four bars, the bass makes its way back to origin. But at the moment when it must land on the octave, the delinquent melody pulls one last shock. It hits and hangs on the note below, a suspended dissonance that threatens to spread perpetually. He wonders if the chord will ever come home.

A change comes over Dr. Koss, too, with the music. No longer the skittish girl filled with punch lines. Legs crossed, neck arched, head tilted, she sheds the sunbather and becomes a *mater dolorosa.* At the aria's end, Ressler, scared by how much empty space has flooded into K-53-C, moves next to her. His entrée to music is exactly this: wanting, just this once, without compromise, to close the curve of this woman's body, the cell surface he has not been able to forget since the moment she took his head in her hands and toweled it dry.

He does not know what she is doing here, why she inflicts this tune on him. She has no personality but the one she adopts this instant. He needs from her precisely this refusal to dissolve into specifics. Whatever he suspects about the motive for her visit disappears somewhere in the thirty-two measures. They sit through the first fifteen variations, rooted a foot from one another. When side one ends, they listen to a few revolutions of dull scratching before either moves. Ressler gets up, flips the record. The fifteen feet of floorboard to the plastic phonograph elongates epically. He fumbles with the cartridge, overwhelmed by aboriginal wonder at the device. All devices.

When he comes back, Koss reaches without looking and puts her arm around his shoulders. She touches his bone blade without hope or threat or promise. A completely unencumbered, uncompromised, just-to-be-touching touch. His shoulders support her arm as if they have known each other since the start. As if they know each other now. As if anyone ever knows the first thing about another.

The piece proceeds, with the modesty of the monumental, to launch an investigation into everything the aria, by permutation, can conceivably become. After an immense journey whose contours he only darkly traces, the piece ends note-for-note as it

began: da capo. Once more, from the head, the delicate filigree of sarabande, fleshed out upon four unfolding scale-steps. When the music stops, they continue to touch immaterially. Olga arabesques on in silence, not knowing the difference. The sinusoidal pulse of the needle scratching the end of the track is surf interrogating the continental coast. The little air and variations, the signal, now dampened, disperses into noise.

A voice calls him back to the world's indifference. "Are you ill? You look febrile." She places the back of her hand on his forehead. He burns to beg her to use that ancient method, instinctive to women: upper-lip thermometer. His temperature would elude even this most heat-sensitive gauge—the burning hotel, plans lost in complexity, night, love's accident, perpetual September, memory, fever beyond telling.

He does not look at her. In another moment, they rise by agreement and walk to the door. Their arms link and unthread. They turn toward one another awkwardly, a gulf of ignorance separating their mutually unreadable faces. Implausible, dead-ended, wrong: he wants only to be rid of her without further calamity. She reaches out, straightens his collar. Do not hate me. Which one of us knows the first thing about what we are after?

"I would like, very much," he begins, but breaks off in an undeserved sense of well-being. Warm air coming off the lawn, the light of his unfurnished army barracks at his back. How cut off, without consequence, they both are from the lights leading out to the black fields on the edge of town. He stands surrounded by danger, experience. "I want . . ." He stops again, unable for the life of him to remember what he wants so badly. The name of the thing.

"I *know*," she giggles, diminished again to teenaged flirt, laughing off the game they have begun, the awful eroticism. There, between them, dispersing as she beats him to the word *goodbye*, is the ladder's base, the replicating heart of the coding problem. What could be simpler? I *know*; I could name that tune in four notes.

On the Runway

I knew an airport security guard who let
me through Gate 47, with eastbound passengers
crossing the Atlantic, out to the landing field

where at the edge of the runway, beyond
the blinking lights, the blue warning
zone, lying in a goldenrod waste of

cement and cracked tar, I waved the night
jets in, quiet in my power, guiding them
down, as they bellied across the bay and

burst with a braking roar, so close
I could feel the engine dust, the
warm asphalt wind in my ears and eyes,

over and over. Every forty-five seconds
gauging their nightweight and speed, I
welcomed the tons of arrival, I the secret

air traffic controller, roused from my
Brooklyn bed to celebrate the might of
souls in commerce, converging, delivered

to my sunken patch of welcome, an almost
underground cell charged with secret
connections to water and darkness. With each

flight down, I could have gladly gone
under for good, etched in granite and
rock, a grateful fossil, a shining

tattoo, last specimen of a species pounded
to sleep in a bedrock of print. As I tried
for some wound long inside to be touched,

if not healed, I craved the jet speed, with
each surge as it came, to become the
pain and then free. But it was hard

to keep faith when the first high failed and
left me crazed and unsure, like a derelict monk
craving the power to bless. Yet it wasn't crazed

to add a slight push or prayer to powers
already there, after prying so long against
them, and it was a wider space to keep watch

than my moonprint pillow. So even if there was,
in my runway vigil, more drama than grace, I stayed
until the first gray, when I left by the gate

I'd come, like a straggler just landed, a late
passenger, grateful to step from a long flight
down onto another quick morning on earth.

Fragments from the
Livro do desassossego

20 December 1932

After the last rains left the sky and remained on the ground—clear sky, earth wet and mirrorlike—the greatest clarity of life, reappearing with the blue above and delighting in the freshness that follows the rain below, left a sky of its own in the soul and a freshness of its own in the heart.

Like it or not, we are slaves of the hour and its colors and forms, subjects of the sky and the earth. Even that part of us that burrows deepest into itself, disdaining its surroundings, does not burrow along the same paths when it rains as when the sky is clear. Obscure transmutations, perhaps sensed only in the intimacy of abstract emotions, take place because it's raining or has stopped raining, are sensed without being sensed, because without our feeling it the weather has made itself felt.

Each of us is various, is many, is a prolixity of selves.

Thus the self who disdains the surrounding environment is not the same one who rejoices or suffers on account of it. In the vast colony of our being, there are people of many species, thinking and feeling differently. In this very moment in which, in a legitimate break from work, which is scarce today, I write down these few impressions, I am the one who is writing attentively, I am the one who is pleased not to have to work just now, I am the one who sees the sky out there, which is invisible from here, I am the one

who is thinking all this, I am the one who is aware of a contented body and hands that are still slightly cold. And this whole world of mine, made up of people who are alien to each other, projects like a disparate but compact multitude a single shadow: this motionless, writing body, with which I stand and lean against Borges's tall desk, where I came to fetch my blotter, which I had lent him.

[Undated]

Today, feeling my body oppressed by that old anxiety that sometimes wells up, I didn't eat well, nor did I drink as much as usual, in the restaurant on whose mezzanine I base the continuation of my existence. And when, as I was leaving, the waiter noticed that the wine bottle was still half full, he turned to me and said, "Goodbye until later, Senhor Soares, and I hope you feel better."

At the clarion call of this simple phrase my soul was relieved as though the wind had suddenly cleared a clouded sky. And then I realized what I had never realized clearly, that in these waiters in cafés and restaurants, in barbers, in the porters stationed on street corners, I find a spontaneous, natural sympathy that I can't pride myself on receiving from those with whom I am, improperly speaking, on more intimate terms . . .

Fraternity has its subtleties.

Some govern the world, others are the world. Between an American millionaire with property in England or Switzerland and the socialist leader of the village, there is no difference of quality, merely one of quantity. We are beneath these men, we, the amorphous ones: the disorderly dramatist William Shakespeare, the schoolmaster John Milton, the vagrant Dante Alighieri, the errand boy who carried my message yesterday, or the barber who tells me jokes, the waiter who just did me the human kindness of hoping I would feel better because he saw I had drunk only half my wine.

8 September 1933

High in the solitude of the night, an unknown lamp blooms behind a window. Everything else in the city that I see is dark, except where faint reflections of light from the streets rise vaguely, creating here and there a hovering inverse

moonlight, very pale. In the black of the night, little stands out of the colors or shades of colors in the block of houses: only slight differences, which one might call abstract, lend irregularity to the flattened mass.

An invisible thread binds me to the lamp's anonymous owner. It is not the common circumstance of our both being awake: there is no possible reciprocity in this, since he could never see me at the window in the darkness. It is something else, concerning me alone, that has to do with the sense of isolation, that partakes of the night and the silence, that chooses that lamp as a resting point because it's the only resting point there is. It seems that the night is so dark because it is lighted. It seems that it shines because I am awake, dreaming in the dark.

Everything that exists exists perhaps because something else exists. Nothing is, everything coexists: perhaps that's right. I sense that I would not exist at this hour—at least not as I am, with this present awareness of myself, which because it is conscious and present is at this moment entirely me—if that lamp were not shining over there, elsewhere, a lighthouse indicating nothing from a false advantage of height. I feel this because I feel nothing. I think this because this is nothing. Nothing, nothing, part of the night and the silence, of what I am that with them is nothing, is negative, is interstice, space between me and myself, substance of the forgetfulness of some god or other.

7 April 1933

I passed among them as a stranger but no one saw that I was one. I lived among them as a spy and nobody, not even I, suspected that I was one. Everyone considered me a relative: no one knew that I had been switched at birth. So I was the same as the others without resembling them, everybody's brother without belonging to the family.

I came from prodigious lands, from landscapes better than life, but I never spoke of the lands except to myself, and of the landscapes seen in dreams I never told anyone. My steps were like those of the others on the floors and the flagstones, but my heart was far away, although it beat close by, false master of a foreign body in exile.

No one knew me behind the mask of equality or ever knew that

it was a mask, because no one knew that there are masqueraders in this world. No one imagined that beside me there was always someone else, who after all was myself. They always thought I was identical to myself.

Their houses sheltered me, their hands shook mine, they saw me passing in the street as though I were there; but who I am was never in those rooms, the one whose life I live has no hands for others to shake, who I know myself to be has no streets to walk, except all streets, and no way of being seen in the streets unless he himself is everyone else.

We all live distant and anonymous; disguised, we suffer unrecognized. To some, however, this distance between a being and himself is never revealed; to others it is illuminated occasionally, in horror or anguish, in a measureless flash; but to others still this is the painful constancy and daily fare of life.

To know that who we are has nothing to do with us, that whatever we think or feel is always a translation, that what we want we did not want, nor, for that matter, did anyone want it— to know all this every minute with every emotion, is this not what it is to be a stranger in one's own soul, exiled in one's own sensations?

But the mask that I was staring at passively, which spoke on the street corner with a maskless man on this last night of Carnival, finally held out his hand and said goodbye, laughing. The natural man turned the corner to the left and went off down the side street. The mask—charmless disguise—walked straight ahead, moving away between shadows and splashes of light, in a definitive parting that was foreign to what I was thinking. Only then did I notice that there was something in the street other than the lighted lamps and, clouding the spaces between them, a vague moonlight, veiled, silent, full of nothing, like life itself . . .

7 October 1931

The sunset spreads on scattered clouds over the whole sky. Reflections of every color, mild reflections, fill the gradations of the upper air, float absently among the great bruises in the sky. On the tall rooftops, half color, half shadow, the last slow rays of the setting sun take on colors that belong neither to them nor to the things they rest on. There is a great calm above

the noisy city, which is also settling into silence. Beyond the color and the sound, everything draws a deep, silent breath.

The colored buildings not touched by the sun begin to take on tones of gray. There is a chill in the diversity of these colors. A slight uneasiness sleeps in the false valleys of the streets. It drowses and settles. And gradually, on the lowest of the high clouds, the reflections turn to shadow; only that tiny cloud, like a white eagle above the rest, retains the smiling gold of the distant sun.

Everything I have sought in life I myself abandoned by seeking it. I am like someone who searches distractedly for something that, in the dream within the search, he has already forgotten. More real than the absent object of the search becomes the actual gesture of the visible hands that search, turning over, displacing, placing; they exist, white and long, with five fingers each, exactly.

Everything I have had is like this high, variously same sky: tatters of nothing touched by a distant light, fragments of false life that death gilds from afar with its sad smile of utter truth. All I have had, yes, has been the ignorance of how to search, feudal lord of marshes at dusk, deserted prince of a city of empty tombs.

All that I am or was, or that I think of what I am or was, all this suddenly loses—in my thoughts and in the high cloud's sudden loss of light—the secret, the truth, the destiny perhaps, that might have lain in whatever underlies life. All this, like a vanished sun, is what remains to me, and on the tall roofs the light variously lets its failing hands slip, and in the unity of the roofs the intimate shadow of everything comes into view.

Vague trembling drop, small in the distance, the first star shines.

15 September 1931

Clouds . . . Today I am conscious of the sky, although there are days when I don't look at it but sense it, living in the city and not in the world of nature that encompasses it. Clouds . . . Today they are the principal reality, and they preoccupy me as though the clouding over of the sky were one of the great dangers of my destiny. Clouds . . . They pass from the river's mouth to the castle, from west to east, in a sparse and scattered tumult, sometimes white, if they are traveling tattered in the vanguard of I don't know what; other times half-black, if they are slow to be swept away by the sounding wind; black with a dirty whiteness

if, as though lingering, they cast a deeper darkness with their appearance than with their shadow on the false perspectives that the streets open up between the blocks' converging lines.

Clouds . . . I exist without knowing it and I'll die without wanting to. I am the interval between what I am and what I am not, between what I dream and what life has made of me, the abstract and corporeal midpoint of things that are nothing, while I too am nothing. Clouds . . . What uneasiness if I feel, what discomfort if I think, what uselessness if I desire! Clouds . . . They are always passing: some very large ones that, because the buildings make it impossible to see whether they are smaller than they appear, seem as though they will take up the whole sky; others of uncertain size, which could be two joined together or one about to divide, directionless in the upper air against the exhausted sky; still others that are small, resembling toys of powerful things, irregular balls from an abstract game, off to one side, in extreme isolation, cold.

Clouds . . . I interrogate myself, and I do not know myself. I have done nothing useful and I shall do nothing that is justifiable. The life that I haven't wasted in the confused interpretation of nothing, I have spent writing prose verses to the untransmissible sensations whereby I make the unknown universe mine. I am fed up with myself, objectively and subjectively. I am fed up with everything and with all of everything. Clouds . . . They are everything, remnants from on high, the only real things today between the earth that is nothing and the heavens that don't exist; indescribable shreds of the tedium I impose on them; fog condensed into threats of absent color; dirty cotton wads from a hospital without walls. Clouds . . . They are like me, a fragmented passage between heaven and earth, at the mercy of an invisible impulse, thunderous or not, gaily white or darkly black, fictions of the interstice and the lost way, far from the noise of the earth and without the silence of the sky.

Clouds . . . They continue passing, continue always passing, they will pass always, continuing, in a discontinuous winding of dense skeins, in a diffuse prolongation of false, fragmented sky.

—Translated by Alice Sedgwick Wohl

Biographical Note

Fernando Pessoa—the name means "person," from the Latin *persona,* or actor's mask—was born in Lisbon in 1888. Much of his early life was spent in Durban, South Africa, where his stepfather was the Portuguese consul. In 1905 Pessoa returned to Lisbon, where he lived until his death in 1935. He had a great impact on the cultural life of Portugal from 1910 on, founding avant-garde movements and periodicals in which the principal artists of the time participated.

He deliberately chose a solitary life and a modest, part-time occupation (as a commercial secretary in import-export firms) in order to devote himself to writing. But only a fraction of his vast oeuvre was published in his lifetime. It appeared mostly in magazines and newspapers, under his own name, Fernando Pessoa, and under his heteronyms, the names of his "other selves." The various distinct and independent voices, to whom he attributed an autonomy that was both biographical and creative, included Fernando Pessoa (author of lyric verses and the esoteric poem *Mensagem* [Message]) and the other Portuguese poets Alberto Caeiro, Alvaro de Campos, and Ricardo Reis; the English poet Alexander Search and the French poet Jean Seul; the philosophers António Mora and Raphael Baldaia; and, finally, the prose writer Bernardo Soares, author of the *Livro do desassossego* (Book of Disquiet).

This posthumous book, which was not published until 1982, is a collection of prose texts written throughout Pessoa's life but never arranged in a definitive form. The texts constitute a diary attributed to Bernardo Soares, a man about thirty years old, tall, thin, and slightly stooped. Although pale, modest, almost anonymous in manner, Soares reveals himself to be unexpectedly cultivated. He is an assistant bookkeeper in a wholesale draper's office, and lives alone in a rented room in the Rua dos Douradores in downtown Lisbon, near the Tagus River. This modest clerk's dismal life has a surprising side to it: in the solitude of his evenings, when he confides his brief notes to his diary, the character of Bernardo Soares is transfigured. Although his notes often start with a banal fact of his banal

Pessoa in Lisbon, 1925

daily life, they proceed powerfully to address such themes as life, death, identity, art, beauty, and above all the relationship between reality and the self.

The *Livro do desassossego* is in the form of a diary, but, as the Italian novelist (and translator of Pessoa) Antonio Tabucchi points out, it is properly called a novel, since Pessoa invented the character, Bernardo Soares, who writes a diary. Thus Soares is "a fictional character who employs the subtle literary fiction of autobiography." While most of Pessoa's other heteronyms are poets, Soares remains steadfastly attached to prose; while the others travel, in poetry or fictitious life, all over the world, Soares never leaves his place of confinement. But, as he says, "there is also a universe in the Rua dos Douradores." Soares knows that even in prison it is possible to sing the song of the infinite.

—Maria José de Lancastre

Disturbed by Freedom

MY HAND IS A GUN AND EACH FINGER
IS A BARREL
and my arm is growing stretching reaching
like a DREAM and I don't know
what to shoot, surely not the robins who have flown
ALL
the way
BACK
from the mountains of Sonora over the desert
where I have driven amazed at the craggy
strangeness of raw beauty.
((THAT'S WHAT I AM ABOUT: BEAUTY
—BEAUTY AND SENSE))
and these robins have alighted here
in these green meadows where sprinkled water
turning warm runs over the masses of pink blooms.
I CANNOT SHOOT THE SOUND OF THE TRAFFIC.
A hundred bullets
would not stop that bus and I
would not hurt the children
or the adolescents at the moving windows
with their pink mohawk haircuts
and their sexual cries
LIKE HUMAN MACAWS.
It is another day and another dollar.
I
WONDER

WHERE

I

AM

((ROAMING SO SWEETLY FROM FIELD

TO FIELD DIS-

TURBED BY MY FREEDOM!))

—AND LOOK AT THE DEEP SCRATCHES THAT MADMEN

make with their keys on the sleek red

lacquer of my car.

I taste coffee in my mouth.

MY MOUTH IS WHERE I AM LIVING TODAY

but I am lonely as a skinny

old white cat with blue eyes

and irregular jagged spots of gray and black

showing a tiger pattern.

I am a tyger, I am an owl. I am some ancient wisdom

taking its own pulse and listening:

BANG!

BANG! goes my finger.

BANG! Lover, I wish

we had bought

the purplish polish for your

toe

nails!

Robert Rauschenberg, *A Doodle (Borealis)*, 1990

Each cover of *Grand Street* features an actual-size detail of a chosen artwork. The entire work is reproduced above. An enlarged detail from the same work appears on the title page. A portfolio of works on paper by Robert Rauschenberg begins on page 57.

CONTRIBUTORS

Grover Amen is a poet, fiction writer, and painter who lives in Brooklyn. His first book of poetry, *F Train Ramble*, was published in 1982. He has just completed a new collection of poetry and a novel, *The Prophet of Bourbon Street.*

Jimmy Santiago Baca was raised by his grandparents, then lived in an orphanage and on the streets for nine years before being arrested. In prison, he began to write poetry, receiving encouragement from Will Inman and Denise Levertov. His books (published by New Directions) include *Martin & Meditations on the South Valley*, which won the 1989 Hispanic Heritage Award; *Black Mesa Poems*; and most recently *Immigrants in Our Own Land & Selected Early Poems*. Baca lives outside Albuquerque. He is currently working on poetry, a novel, and screenplays.

Linda Connor's photographs have been represented in many exhibitions, including one-person shows at the Art Institute of Chicago, the Graham Gallery in Houston, and Gallery Min in Tokyo. Her exhibition "Spiral Journey" is currently traveling around the country; the book *Spiral Journey* was published by the Museum of Contemporary Photography in Chicago. Connor teaches at the San Francisco Art Institute.

Julio Cortázar, the Argentinian author, died in 1984. His short story collections include *The End of the Game, All Fires the Fire, Cronopios and Famas,* and *Around the Day in Eighty Worlds. Hopscotch* is his best-known novel; his others include *The Winners, 62: A Model Kit,* and *A Certain Lucas.* Cortázar translated the works of Edgar Allan Poe and Marguerite Yourcenar's *Memoirs of Hadrian* into Spanish.

Sarah Gorham is the author of *Don't Go Back to Sleep*, published by Galileo Press in 1989. Recent poems have appeared or will appear in *Poetry, The Kenyon Review, Ploughshares,* and *Poetry Northwest.* Gorham was the 1990 winner of PNW's Carolyn Kizer Award and a 1991 recipient of a Kentucky Foundation for Women grant.

André Gorz is a heretic French social thinker. His latest books are *Farewell to the Working Class* (South End Press, 1982), *Paths to Paradise* (South End Press, 1985), and *Critique of Economic Reason* (Verso, 1989).

George Hixson, born in New York in 1956, lives and works in Houston as a fine art photographer and illustrator.

Mari Hoashi is completing work toward an M.A. degree in East Asian Studies at Columbia University, where she also received an M.S. degree in Journalism. She is a reporter on NHK TV.

John Hollander teaches at Yale. His most recent book of poems is *Harp Lake*, published by Knopf. This spring Yale University Press is reissuing his book of pattern poems, *Types of Shape*, in an expanded edition with commentary.

Kazuo Ishiguro was born in Japan. When he was five, he moved with his family to England, where he has lived ever since. His first novel, *A Pale View of Hills*, was awarded the Royal Society of Literature Prize; his second, *An Artist of the Floating World*, received the Whitbread Book of the Year Award; and his latest, *The Remains of the Day*, won the 1989 Booker Prize.

John Keane is Director of the Centre for the Study of Democracy and Professor of Politics at the Polytechnic of Central London. He is the author of many books, including *Public Life and Late Capitalism* (1984), *Democracy and Civil Society* (1988), and *The Media and Democracy* (1991), and is at present completing a biography of Tom Paine.

Maria José de Lancastre is a professor of Portuguese literature at the University of Pisa. With her husband, Antonio Tabucchi, she has translated all of Fernando Pessoa into Italian. Her *Pessoa: Une photobiographie* was published in 1990 by Christian Bourgois éditeur.

CONTRIBUTORS

Alberto Manguel is a reviewer, translator, and anthologist. His first novel, *News From a Foreign Country Came*, was published by Clarkson Potter in April.

Herbert Woodward Martin is a Fulbright Lecturer at Janus Pannonius University, Pecs, Hungary, for 1990–91. He has been invited by the Yugoslavian government to lecture there on American and Afro-American poetry. His poems have appeared in *Poetry, The Beloit Poetry Journal*, and *Ploughshares*. He is poet in residence at the University of Dayton, in Ohio.

New Directions has just published *Rebel Lions*, a collection of new poems by **Michael McClure**. McClure is performing at colleges and music venues with the Doors' keyboardist Ray Manzarek: he reads his poetry while Manzarek plays piano. Mystic Fire Video will release a video of their performance.

Masao Miyoshi is Hajime Mori Professor of Japanese, English, and Comparative Literature at the University of California, San Diego. His book *Off Center: Power and Culture Relations Between Japan and the United States* will be published by Harvard University Press later this year.

Peter Nagy was born in 1959. He lives and works in New York. He is represented by Jay Gorney Modern Art and Jablonka Galerie in Cologne.

The novelist **Kenzaburo Oe** was born in 1935 on the remote Japanese island of Shikoku. Of his many novels, *The Silent Cry*, *A Personal Matter*, and *Teach Us to Outgrow Our Madness* have been translated into English.

Eric Ormsby's poems have appeared in various magazines, including *Chelsea, The New Yorker*, and *Shenandoah*. His collection *Bavarian Shrine and Other Poems* (Toronto: ECW

Press) appeared in 1990. "Mutanabbi in Exile" is from a new collection of poems on classical Arabic themes, entitled *Mutanabbi.*

Other writings of **Fernando Pessoa** available in English include *Poems of Fernando Pessoa* (Ecco) and, as "Alberto Caeiro," *The Keeper of Sheep* (Sheep Meadow), both translated by Susan Brown and Edwin Honig. For biographical information, see the note that follows "Fragments from the *Livro do desassossego.*"

Richard Powers is the author of *Three Farmers on the Way to a Dance* and *Prisoner's Dilemma.* "We Are Climbing Jacob's Ladder" is an excerpt from his forthcoming novel, *The Gold Bug Variations,* which will be published by William Morrow & Co.

In 1982, **Robert Rauschenberg** began a unique project and touring exhibition: the Rauschenberg Overseas Cultural Interchange (ROCI). The project involved Rauschenberg's intensive collaboration with indigenous artists and craftsmen throughout ROCI's eight-year tour of twelve countries including Mexico, Venezuela, China, Japan, Sri Lanka, Cuba, and the USSR. A major selection of this work will be shown in the summer of 1991 at the National Gallery of Art in Washington, D.C. He is represented by Knoedler Gallery, New York.

Aaron Shurin's books include *The Graces* (Four Seasons Foundation), *A's Dream* (O Books), a recent chapbook of prose, *Narrativity,* and a forthcoming collection, *Into Distances,* both from Sun & Moon Press. He teaches at San Francisco State University and City College of San Francisco.

Ben Sonnenberg was editor of *Grand Street* from 1981 to spring 1990. "Upstaged" is taken from *Lost Property: Memoirs & Confessions of a Bad Boy,* to be published in May by Summit Books.

CONTRIBUTORS

Amy Tan is the author of *The Joy Luck Club.* "Peanut's Fortune" is an excerpt from her second book, *The Kitchen God's Wife,* which will be published by G. P. Putnam's Sons.

Chris Turner is a freelance translator and writer who lives and works in Birmingham, England. His work includes translations of Jean Baudrillard, Philippe Lacoue-Labarthe, and Klaus Theweleit.

Rosanna Warren is the author of *Each Leaf Shines Separate,* a book of poems, and has edited and contributed to *The Art of Translation: Voices From the Field.* She is completing a biography of Max Jacob and a translation of Euripides' *The Suppliants.*

Alice Sedgwick Wohl has translated Fernão Lopes's *Crónica de D. Pedro I* and the *Vita di Michelangelo Buonarroti* by Ascanio Condivi, as well as other shorter works. She is now working on a critical edition, in English, of Giovanni Pietro Bellori's *Vite de' pittori, scultori e architetti moderni.*

Charles Wright is the author of ten books of poems and three books of translations. His most recent book of poems is *The World of the Ten Thousand Things: Poems 1980–1990,* published by Farrar, Straus & Giroux. He lives in Charlottesville, Virginia.

ILLUSTRATIONS

cover & title page Robert Rauschenberg, *A Doodle (Borealis)* (details), 1990, acrylic and tarnishes on brass, 72¾ x 96¾ in. Courtesy of the artist.

p. 17 Tan family friends, Shanghai, c. 1930s. Courtesy of Amy Tan.

p. 30 Sonnenberg home, 19 Gramercy Park (detail). Photograph by Steven Tucker.

p. 35 Photograph by Steven Tucker.

p. 40 George Hixson, untitled, 1991, solarized gelatin silver print, 10 x 8 in.

pp. 59, 61, 65, 67, 71 Robert Rauschenberg, five drawings (titles accompany illustrations), 1991, acrylic on paper, 45 x 35 in. Courtesy of the artist.

pp. 62–63, 68–69 Robert Rauschenberg, two drawings (titles accompany illustrations), 1991, acrylic on paper, 45 x 70 in. Courtesy of the artist.

pp. 74, 79 Photographs by Kazumi Kurigami. Courtesy of *Switch*.

p. 85 Photograph by Naoki Matsumoto. Courtesy of *Switch*.

p. 116 Peter Nagy, *Léger* (Cancer Logo series), 1985, photocopy of master image employed in paintings of various scales. Courtesy of the artist.

pp. 117, 118–19 (detail) Peter Nagy, *To Die Alive*, 1990, enamel on steel, 51 x 48 in. Edition of three and artist's proof. Courtesy of Jay Gorney Modern Art.

p. 120 Peter Nagy, *America Invented Everything* (Cancer Logo series), 1985, photocopy of master image. Courtesy of the artist.

pp. 121, 122–23 (detail) Peter Nagy, *Urbanism and the Call to Prayer*, 1990, enamel on steel, 36¾ x 46¼ in. Edition of three and artist's proof. Courtesy of Jay Gorney Modern Art.

p. 124 Peter Nagy, *Parasitical Clown Dough* (Cancer Logo series), 1986, photocopy of master image. Courtesy of the artist.

pp. 125, 126–27 (detail) Peter Nagy, *You Adore Me*, 1990, enamel on steel, 36 x 36 in. Edition of four. Courtesy of Jay Gorney Modern Art.

ILLUSTRATIONS

p. 130 Courtesy of Bettmann Archive.

p. 136 Lewis Hine, *Steamfitter,* 1921, gelatin silver photograph, 10 x 8 in.

p. 143 Robert Frank, *Assembly Line, Detroit,* 1955, gelatin silver photograph, 7⅝ x 11⅞ in. Courtesy of Pace-MacGill Gallery, New York. Photograph provided by the Museum of Fine Arts, Houston: Target Collection of American Photography.

p. 152 Automated assembly line, NeXT Computer, Inc., Fremont, California. Photograph by Terrence McCarthy/ *NYT Pictures.*

p. 163 ARC Mate Sr. (robotic arc welder). Courtesy of GMFanuc Robotics.

pp. 169-76 Linda Connor, eight photographs (titles p. 177), 1989, negatives contact-printed with sunlight on printing-out paper, 8 x 10 in. Courtesy of the artist.

p. 182 Piano courtesy of Steinway & Sons. Double helix courtesy of Cold Spring Harbor Laboratory Archives.

p. 206 Manuel S. Cabanas, *Fernando Pessoa,* woodcut, c. 1917. Courtesy of Maria José de Lancastre.

p. 214 Photographer unknown. Courtesy of Maria José de Lancastre.

p. 228 Phony money ads, New York City streets.

In our previous issue, *Grand Street* 37, the deck of cards in the photograph (*Poker Hand* by John McIntosh) featured on the cover, the title page, and p. 235 is from *Artdeck: The Game of Modern Masters,* manufactured by Aristoplay, Ltd.

228